Modern Educational Technology

Modern Educational Technology

Anuradha Sharma

Commonwealth

Modern Educational Technology

Edition : 2026

ISBN 81-7169-574-4

Published by :
COMMONWEALTH PUBLISHERS (P) LTD.
4831/24, Govind Lane,
Ansari Road, Darya Ganj,
New Delhi - 110002
Ph. : 23272541, 23242541
e-mail : commonwealthpublishers2016@gmail.com

Distributed by :
ARJUN PUBLISHING HOUSE
4831/24, Govind Lane,
Ansari Road, Darya Ganj,
New Delhi - 110002
Ph. : 23272541, 23242541
e-mail : arjunbooks2001@gmail.com

Laser Typesetting by :
Dimple Computers
Delhi

Printed at :
Milan Enterprises
Delhi

Preface

Educational technology is sometimes too narrowly thought of as confined to hardware, closed-circuit television or language laboratories represent to many educators the sum total of instructional technology—making it very easy to discuss or dismiss. Actually, much more is involved in the concept. If the point of view is taken that the institution of education is now the subject of/and is moving into the general scientific-technological revolution, then hardware, material systems of organization, and new roles for teachers and administrators are all a part of educational technology. Within this broad umbrella, there are subtechnologies; for example, psychological testing, the development of new hardware and the creation of whole systems of materials etc.

When education is viewed as an institution, technology of a sophisticated type can play a part in the management and operation of the entire enterprise. Data processing machinery and techniques are being used for scheduling, pupil accounting, etc.; modular construction of school buildings is being tried; information storage and retrieval processes are being considered as applicable to age-old library problems. There are, in addition, economic and other aspects to this general concept of educational technology. These will, in this paper, be interwoven as the discussion crisscrosses between education as an institution and as a process. The general emphasis, however, will be on the subtechnologies most closely related to instruction, as it is felt that this is the current interest of the Commission These include hardware, materials, systems, organization, and psychological applications.

As technological patterns of thinking and processing invade the previously primitive educational culture, it is inevitable that a drive for systematization should begin.

Editor

Contents

1

Emerging Trends in Educational Technology

The chapter on the emerging technology analyses and summaries the current situation. Finn sees the period in America and applicable to India as one for consolidation of gains in instructional technology but with new developments in the political, social, economic sphere. America has passed through Scientific technological revolution. Education in the United States can be viewed as an institution—social, political, economic. It can also be viewed as a process whereby humans learn and are taught. Subject matter content or skills are also sometimes loose referents to the word "education," in the sense of such phrases as scientific education, physical education, or teacher education. Finally, there is always a definition which represents a description of the effect of personal experiences, as in the classic Education of Henry Adams, or in such a phrase as "that experience taught me a lesson in human relations."

These separate but somewhat overlapping concepts suggest that care need be taken when addressing the problem of the relationships of technology to education. It would appear that the Commission should be interested in the bearings that technology has on education as an institution, a process, and its content. There is also some disagreement within the educational profession as to what is meant by the expression educational technology. A group of experimental psychologists would like to confine the term to an empirical approach to the process of teaching and learning. That is, they refer to the work in experimental psychology as a developing science of learning, and applications of this science for example, applying the principles of operant conditioning to teaching through programmed instruction as the "technology of instruction."

While these psychologists admit that there is, by no means, a one-to-one relationship between their version of the science of learning and the technology of instruction, they view this relationship as the ultimate goal. There are some real weaknesses to this point of view and it will not be the one from which this paper is written. However, since the relationship does exist to some extent, it will be considered within a broader context of educational technology.

Educational or instructional technology is sometimes too narrowly thought of as confined to hardware. Thus, for example, closed-circuit television or language laboratories represent to many educators the sum total of instructional technology—making it very easy to discuss or dismiss. Actually, much more is involved in the concept. If the point of view is taken that the institution of education in the United States is now the subject of and is moving into the general scientific-technological revolution, then hardware, material systems of organization, and new roles for teachers and administrators are all a part of educational technology. Within this broad umbrella, there are subtechnologies; for example, psychological testing, the development of new hardware such as the cartridge-loading 8 mm film viewers, and the creation of whole systems of materials such as those designed for the Physical Science Study Committee by Professor Jerrold Zacharias to teach high school physics.

Further, when education is viewed as an institution, technology of a sophisticated type can (and is, to a small extent, beginning to) play a part in the management and operation of the entire enterprise. For example, data processing machinery and techniques are being used for scheduling, pupil accounting, etc.; modular construction of school buildings is being tried; information storage and retrieval processes are being considered as applicable to age-old library problems. There are, in addition, economic and other aspects to this general concept of educational technology. These will, in this paper, be interwoven as the discussion crisscrosses between education as an institution and as a process. The general emphasis, however, will be on the subtechnologies most closely related to instruction, as it is felt that this is the current interest of the Commission These include hardware, materials, systems, organization, and psychological applications.

Since World War II the national concern with education has been increasing, a concern that took a quantum jump with the unveiling of the first Sputnik. Since that time, the national effort to improve the education system has redoubled several times. However, from the point of view of instructional technology, all concerns cannot be said to originate in the space race. The efforts of the Ford Foundation in the development and promotion of educational television, for example, antedated Sputnik I by several years. The concerns for education represent a sort of catalog of problems and issues relating to instructional technology. These can be briefly listed

1. The population explosion with all it implies in terms of more students and fewer teachers and the necessity for new educational arrangements.
2. The information explosion, which presents great problems in curriculum construction and requires

greater efforts in increasing the erficiency of teaching and learning .

3. The general rising throughout the world, including the United States, of the depressed sectors of mankind. Education is seen as the main weapon in the war on poverty, for example, and the requirements of such an educational war include new methods and techniques to reach these people—here and overseas.

4. The urge to raise the quality of life for all, which, in turn, requires raising the quality of education even though the institution is pressed on all sides by population, knowledge and various kinds of special demands. This situation also sets a requirement, although in a different way, for a more efficient educational process.

5. Research and development of all aspects of education have generated more knowledge about the process and the institution as part of the general knowledge explosion. From this situation rises a drive to introduce all kinds of innovations most of them relating to instructional technology into the educational system. Practice in education has, until the last few years, lagged about 50 years behind research and theory. Today the process of educational innovation itself is under study in an effort to speed up the rate of change.

6. The need for education and re-education and for training and retraining of manpower to meet individual personal needs and national needs increases as society becomes more automated and technologically sophisticated. If, as is often said these days, an individual may have to learn several jobs in a lifetime, the same problems of educational efficiency involving Possible uses of instructional

technology arise—both on a formal and an informal basis.

7. The ill-defined drive toward a new value system, symbolized by the student revolts at Berkely and elsewhere and by very personal concerns on the par' of a segment of the intellectual community, suggests, among other things, dissatisfaction with the abstract, status-oriented, large-scale organization of the college and university characteristic of a technological culture. Since a return to the colonial college is impossible, solutions to these problems, too, must be found in technology, although the student spokesmen would not understand this. The effort to find on of a technological answer, however is a function of a technological society as noted by such students of 'technology as Ellul

There is a cluster of economic pressures pushing for more technology in education. Several foundations, particularly the Ford Foundation, have poured money into the system for developments in this area. The drive to diversify on the part of the aerospace and defense industries as part of the general move into the public sector is another little understood aspect of this problem.

No claim is made that the catalog above is complete or that the application of technology to the educational system or to instruction will solve all the problems listed. It is true, however, that a component of educational technology will have to be present in any attempt at a broad solution. It would, perhaps, be well to examine some of the dimensions of instructional technology as it has developed in order better to understand its possibilities.

For the problem at hand, it is crucial to understand the history of the development of instructional technology for the last 50 years. However, the interested scholar may chase this development back much further than the overworked Greeks, if he desires. The great Sumerologist Samuel Noah Kramer puts the invention of writing on clay tablets at Sumer at about 5,000 years ago and then notes that "The Sumerian school was the direct outgrowth of the invention and development of the cuneiform system of writing". To some extent, the development of devices and techniques of communication the development of a technology of instruction—has affected education ever since. Skipping over thousands of years, the history of 19th century American education is replete with effective technological developments—including the development of textbooks (to which there was some objection), the blackboard, and even improvements in pens and ink. However, from the point of view of the Commission, the crucial period has been roughly from the turn of the century.

The last 60 or 70 years have been marked by social historians as the period of the so-called communications revolution stream-driven rotary presses, photography, motion pictures, radio, etc., with accompanying developments in psychology, mass communication techniques, school organization and finance, etc. The following discussion will break down some of these developments to aid in obtaining perspective.

The best date to mark the beginning of the modem trend of using audiovisual devices and materials in education is about 1920. Before that time, the glass slide, the phonograph record, and to a very limited extent, the 35 mm motion picture had been in some use. After 1920 developments speeded up, partly due to the use of films during World War I. By 1926, 16 mm safety film and equipment for education were available, and a start had been made by the Eastman Kodak Co., in producing educational films; radio had reached its commercial stage and a beginning had been made with educational radio;

other devices and materials were either developed or improved. Another big change—perhaps the big change—came in the middle 30s with the development of the 16 mm sound motion picture, the workhorse of the audiovisual movement.

Accompanying these hardware and material developments had been parallel developments in the study of learning from audiovisual materials, beginning with the first studies made right after World War I by K.S. Lashley and John B. Watson, the great experimental psychologists of their day. This connection between some very able research psychologists, students of mass media, etc., and the audiovisual field has continued to the present and has resulted in a respectable literature, much of which is unknown to general educationists, other psychologists, and to many vocal subject matter experts outside the field of education. It is also safe to say that while these developments did occur partly through the generosity of the Carnegie and Rockefeller Foundations—the application to American educational practice was very limited. There were, for example, only slightly over 600 sound motion picture projectors in the schools of this country in 1936.

By the time the United States entered World War 11, an instructor could have had an adequate instrumentation at his disposal. It included still and motion projectors of several varieties, recording devices and players, various forms of printing, chart production, etc. and sound and communication equipment. In addition, a fair amount of material to use with this equipment was available, and quite a lot of know-how derived from research and practice was at hand In fact, however, very few American school teachers had even seen much of this technology, let alone having it available.

The wide—almost saturated—use of audiovisual materials in the military and industrial training programs during World War 11 has been well told in several places. This was the first successful mass application of the technology of instruction to the training of large groups of men and women.

Following the war, a renewed interest arose in the American public schools in the use of audiovisual materials. Some states, such as California, made a great effort and supplied funds in quantity for this development. Across the United States, however, the reaction was spotty, and the additional know-how derived from the war effort had little effect in many places. In the meantime, hardware developments added to the impetus and the confusion. The development of wire and then magnetic tape recording, the long-playing record, improvements in the optics of projection equipment, and the adoption of the overhead transparency projector which had been developed during the war all contributed. Producers rushed in to turn out motion pictures, recordings, filmstrips, slide sets. Research—some of it financed by the armed services in the problems of learning from these materials was carried on. However, as we approached the middle of the decade of 1950-59, educational interest in what has come to be called conventional audiovisual materials tailed off somewhat. Present developments date from that time and will be discussed below.

Even a brief account of the history subsumed under the title above could fill one or more volumes. The intention here will be merely to outline some of these related developments. The work of Thorndike at Teachers College, Columbia, early in this century set the stage for the development of a scientific psychology of education. Thorridike even anticipated teaching machines and programmed learning. S.L. Pressey of Ohio State University, as is well known, discovered certain principles of machine instruction white attempting to produce a test scoring machine in the 20s.

In the early days of modern educational psychology, there was a tight connection between laboratory experimental psychology and educational practice. Gradually this connection eroded. The experimental psychologists shut themselves up in their laboratories. Some educational psychologists turned their attention to psychological, achievement and other forms of testing and developed a formidable subtechnology that has been the object of some recent criticism. Others turned to the field of guidance. The effect on practice, however, was highly variable. By 1955, this trend toward separation of experimental psychology and practice reversed somewhat and added a forceful element to the developing educational technology. This, too, will be discussed below under the present state of the art.

In the meantime, other research workers, principally in the field of social psychology, had turned their attention to the mass media of communication. The work of Paul Lazarsfeld both before and after World War II is an example. This, together with the work of communication and perception theorists and industrial psychologists interested in group dynamics, had certain fallout value for educational practice. An educational technology began to develop in the group field which had quite 'a vogue until the middle 50s. The work of the mass communication specialists and perception psychologists has had some effect on the theory back of the educational use of audiovisual materials.

With respect to the process of education itself—learning and teaching taking place in an institutional setting—theorists in the 20s had great hope of developing something called "educational engineering". The great leader of this movement was W.W. Charters of Ohio State University. Charters' ideas were attacked and pretty well demolished during the 30s by both the social reform and the child-centered philosophers during the 30s by both the social reform and the child-centered philosophers of education. From the middle 50s onward, the Charters concepts were revived, although in a new form and were seldom attributed to him. Interestingly enough, Charters also had a great interest in audiovisual communication and founded the Institute for Education by Radio and Television at Ohio State in the 30s.

Industrial developments relating to a technology of education can be briefly discussed with reference to (a) the design, development and marketing of hardware and environments, (b) the production and distribution of materials Of instruction, and (c) intra-industry use of instructional technology. Generally speaking, hardware; at least until very recently, has not been designed for use in schools. A manufacturer would produce, for example, a motion picture projector designed for the industrial, home or military market, Small changes might be made for the school market, but the design and reliability needs of educators went unheeded There was many a tragic joke about the 110-pound school teacher who had to carry a 45-pound projector up three flights of stairs. The whole question of the design of instructional equipment is discussed in a paper of the Technological Development Project of the NEA. Badly designed equipment and equipment mismatched to educational needs were among the causes for the failure of schools to rush to adopt innovations during the postwar period.

School buildings provide spaces for learning—learning environments. As such, they are part of the technology that should aid in learning and obviously should be matched with other technologies that have the same end. Since before World War II, this had not been true. Recently, some signs of change are evident School architects have done a pretty good job in providing space for certain special educational functions——gymnasium, auditoriums, shops, etc. They have, over the last 30 years, immensely improved the aesthetic quality of the school environment—color, light, etc. They have made the environment more healthful with such things as better lighting and ventilation. They have done almost nothing to help the general instructional process by providing for modem instructional technology. Until recently, the concentration on using natural lighting through acres of glass windows has prevented full use of projection equipment, and many schools today still do not have adequate light control, acoustic treatment, or wiring. Beginning about 1955, this situation too, has changed for the better.

Problems of the design of instructional equipment over the last 50 years and, to a certain extent, problems of the design of buildings are inextricably related to the economics of education The manufacturer could not invest the necessary capital to create special educational equipment because his chances of recovery in a reasonable time were almost nil. The manufacturer, therefore, adapted existing commercial equipment and made very few changes in the fundamental models marketed for educational use once they were set. One manufacturer used the same stampings for the body of a projector for about 20 years, ignoring both the needs of the teacher and the technological developments that had occurred during that time.

The economic problems involved in providing an educational technology during this period were complex. The educational establishment had no precedent and no great inclination for investing in a machine technology at all. The local and state system of finance left little money in educational coffers for investment in technological capital. The local nature of the educational market together with local bidding procedures prevented large-scale selling. The distribution organizations of the manufacturers were primitive, ranging from one-man camera and music stores to a few large audiovisual dealers with service departments.

The materials side of the developing educational technology over the same period also suffered from a lack of market on the part of the schools and a lack of capital, vigour and imagination on the part of the producers. The first three large-scale efforts to produce educational films were subsidized for many years by industry—partly in the hope of eventually developing a profitable market and partly for what have to philanthropic reasons. Eastman Kodak subsidized Eastman Teaching Films in the 20s; Western Electric subsidized ERPI 'Classroom Films beginning in the 30s and running for about 20 years; David Smart began producing Coronet Films on his own estate, using the profits of Esquire.

The textbook market, while no doubt profitable over the same period of time, never realized its potential School systems sometimes kept the same textbooks in use for periods as long as 25 years—with all that implies in terms of outdated learning. It is only very recently that the development of libraries for elementary schools has taken hold, and many junior high school and high school libraries still are pretty bad.

In 1948, the textbook industry had a study made by a consulting firm to see if the industry should expand generally into the audiovisual field. The conclusion was that it should not. McGraw-Hill, a firm that had already made a beginning in this direction, ignored the recommendations and now occupies a commanding position as an overall producer of all kinds of teaching materials. In general, the publishing industry is still not facing up to the general technological developments that are occurring.

As more of the newer media—long-playing records, tapes, etc.—came in, the same marketing procedures applied. The supply a school had of new and older materials could only be said to be fortuitous; it often depended upon who called on the superintendent. Maps had to be obtained by mail order or from a salesman who worked a large territory out of his house; the supply of textbooks depended upon the vagaries of state law—in Kansas students had to buy them, but in California they were supplied free; the demand for films, slides, filmstrips, etc. was conditioned upon equipment available and the extent of library service; this is a classic chicken-egg situation and is, incidentally, one faced with the introduction of any new media or technology of instruction

Beginning with the National Defense Education Act in 1958, the general marketing picture changed radically and with it improvements in the overall technological capital of the 'educational system. Figures available to 1960, however, indicate that the technological capital of the American education system is still in a primitive stage; I have suggested that the Rostow concept of five stages of technological growth of a primitive society can be applied to the educational system and that the American educational system may be about ready for technological "takeoff"

Some time and space have been spent on this very sketchy account of the development of some aspects of educational technology in American education in this century because many educated laymen are not aware of these developments. Many seem to assume that the concept of educational technology sprang full blown from the forehead of B.F. Skinner about 1954, or began when the Ford Foundation blessed instructional television with money the same year. To some degree, judgements as to what will and should happen with educational technology have to be conditioned on its history—even if every decision made up to this point in time has to be reversed.

These developments, set arbitrarily from 1955, have led us to the present time. All the evidence suggests that the, middle of the 50s marked a shift, a quantum jump, in technological development for American education. This shift brings us to the present state of the art, and it will be described in the following section.

As was indicated above, the year 1955 has been arbitrarily et as the beginning of modem developments in instructional technology that have given rise to such expressions as "the technological revolution in education". This period was examined in some detail by me in 1960. A brief overview of developments in the 10-year period after 1955 should provide a reasonable description of the state of the art.

Hardware

More or less all technological developments during this time—machines, materials, techniques, organization patterns, etc.—may be conveniently classified into two large categories:

1. A technology of mass or large-group instruction.
2. A technology of individual instruction.

Developments in instructional hardware fall neatly into these categories. Television is the instrument per excellence of mass education, even if the receiver is watching alone. The promoters of educational television in the beginning viewed television as an instrument designed to help solve the teacher shortage by providing quality instruction with fewer teachers. Television may be either broadcast, closed-circuit or broadcast on the 2500 mg band. There are now about 100 educational television stations in the United States. The tendency in recent years is for these stations to transmit more cultural programs and more program of a general educational nature for both adults and preschool children. School broadcasting (instructional television) still occupies some time on these channels. For reception, there were about 50,000 television receivers in the schools in 1962.

Closed-circuit television and the adoption of the 2500 mg band provide a more direct means for using television in school instruction. The adoption of closed-circuit television has not been spectacular. As of 1963, there were approximately 600 such illustrations of all kinds in schools and colleges in the United States.

Related to television development has been the development of the video-tape recorder. In the beginning, the price was prohibitive for educational channels, but the Ford Foundation eventually supplied the nation's educational television stations with professional video-tape recorders. In the last five years, efforts, including competition from the Japanese, tended to reduce the size, complexity and price of equipment. There are still problems of broadcast comparability. Video-tape recording, of course permits the freezing, storage and free scheduling of television instruction.

The other large development has been the language laboratory, a sophisticated combination of sound equipment centering on the tape recorder, now often called the learning laboratory. The language laboratory is a device making it possible to drill many students in speaking and listening at the same time as individuals. Further, since there are oral aspects to other subject and skill areas, the possibilities of expanding the use of such a facility are being explore : many places. There are about 10,000 units in the United States, making this development the most spectacular from the point of view of adoption and expenditure of funds. These laboratories range all the way from small portable units that can be set on a table or wheeled around on a cart to very large and complex installations.

A third technological approach to a large-group instruction is called multimedia, or multi-media/multi-screen. Here the hardware innovations are in the form of control equipment which can operate several different types of projectors, projecting on two or more persons, singly or together Projection may be from the rear, as in the case of the Multi-Media Laboratory of the University of Wisconsin, or from the front, as in the case of a system developed at the University of Southern California. This technique permits the projection of slides, motion pictures, and overhead transparencies as well as the playing of tapes and recordings, very often with teachers or lectures playing an integral part in the presentation.

There have been small improvements in other forms of mass instructional technology as the conventional audiovisual devices have undergone some development, as, for example, the semiautomatic threading 16 mm motion picture projector and the semiautomatic or automatic slide projector. In some ways, principally due to improvements in the equipment which made it much easier to use and to a superb approach to marketing by one large company, the Minnesota Mining and Manufacturing Co., the overhead transparency projector has now become a great contender for the educational technological innovation of the decade, after languishing since its development from the bowling alley projector by the Navy in 1941. Coupled with the tremendous increase in the equipment has been a tremendous increase in eggs or chickens, as the case may be. Transparency materials of all kinds, some prepared transparencies, some materials making it easy for teachers to prepare, and some sort of in between arrangements, like cake mix, have become available. By far the most widely used process recently has been the heat-transfer office copy machine since transparent materials have been developed to use with it.

Principally due to publicity, the technology of individual instruction is thought by many to center on the teaching machine. This is not the case. When B.F. Skinner published his famous article in Science in 1958, a great interest developed in teaching machines and programmed learning. This interest not only engaged psychologists, but also segments of industry from small inventors to large firms. From late 1959 to 1962, a rash of companies went into the teaching machine business.. Most of the small ones have disappeared and most of the large ones have dropped the projects.

This situation had several causes, The educational community was hardly ready for such a startling innovation, the whole business suffered from the same old chicken-egg situation There were not enough program for the machines; the machines were not standardized so that one program could fit another; most machines were poorly designed; most programs violated all principles of programming. Research showed no difference between machine and book-type programs. Programmed instruction survived in the form of books, notebooks and other ways of using printed material without machines and is, at present, the captive of publishers who are not particularly interested in a machine approach.

The teaching machine, however, is not dead. Some experimentation continues across the country. In a few places, third and fourth generation machines have been produced. The basic problem in the early days was that teaching machines attempted to present verbal information only. This was all that most programmers knew how to prepare. The capability of a machine, however, is in the direction, on the one hand, of a complex stimulus—picture, sound, color, as well as words—and, on the other, of a complex response mechanism relating the student's response instantaneously to the task at hand.

In addition to teaching machines per se, a range of devices is in use or development that constitutes a solid technology of individual instruction. Using phonograph records and, later, magnetic tape, some teachers began experimenting with "listening corners" in the elementary school shortly after World War II. Headphones on gang jacks were developed so that several children could list ten at once without disturbing the class. Later, illustrative materials in the form of filmstrips and slides and various kinds of workbooks and directions were added. A short of home grown individual instructional technology was developed in a few places

Following on the heels of this, several manufacturers brought out well-designed listening and viewing devices for filmstrips, tapes, sound film strips, etc. The materials producers have not kept up with this development too well, although they have produced some materials. A lot of work remains to be done to produce the proper kind of material for individual as opposed to group use.

However, the most significant development on the individual instructional technology front has been the growth of 8mm film. About 1960, sound was added successfully to 8mm film, this event triggered a large number of developments in 8mm, many of them, interestingly enough, in the silent field. Although 8 mm may be projected for fairly large groups and, with the new format just announced, will probably generate a projected image about as good as 16mm. was 10 to 15 years ago, it is in the field of individual instruction that 8mm seems to be destined to make its mark. The small, inexpensive technicolor cartridge-loading projector for individual viewing is already finding much use and has started a new materials movement known as "the single concept film". The single concept film is a two-or three-minute film on a self-winding cartridge that may be inserted in the projector and be ready to project. It covers a single idea; for example, nuclear fission. The Air Force recently ordered a quantity of these projectors with stop-frame devices which make it possible to program the films and use the projector somewhat as a teaching machine. Viewing devices for 8mm sound film are also coming on the Market. What this will do to television is still not clear, especially since there are other developments in the video-tape recording field that bear on the problem of individual viewing and listening.

In the last five years, a great deal has been heard about the "systems approach" in education. This interest has increased recently; there are projects at Syracuse University, Michigan State University, and the University of Southern California that are working on certain aspects of the problem, The systems concept in education is related both to materials and to hardware as well as to certain psychological and philosophical concepts.

Technically, if you consider such expressions as the educational system, the school system, and the state system of higher education, then an instructional system is a subsystem. It is this subsystem that is generally the object of the systems approach in education.

One way to understand the developing instruction system is to approach it through the materials of instruction. In this sense, the idea is not too new; for example, with the introduction of graded teachers accompanied ,v workbooks, etc. in the 20s, a sort of system of teaching reading was introduced into the schools. However, the decade we are examining has been a speeding up of trends toward systematic organization of the materials of instruction. This trend was identified by the Technological Development Project of the NEA as "from its to systems". There are now available all sorts of kits for teachers to use which consist of a variety of materials organized around a topic, such as the country, a process, or a concept. These kits often include paperback books, filmstrips, realia, phonograph records or tapes, etc. The kit is accompanied by a manual which suggests how the resources may be deployed.

Another systematic approach to instruction began several years ago with the production of a whole series of film lessons in the field of physics. This was followed by other film series in other areas. These were not simply "aids". They were systematic presentations of content accompanied by suggestions for other activities and related, to some degree, to texts or other materials.

The concept of the Physical Science Study Committee project under the direction of Professor Zacharias developed an even more systematic approach. Here, beginning with a thorough textbook revision, laboratory exercises, an apparatus, a whole film series, and some other materials were prepared. This development was accompanied by tryouts in the schools and a program in the summer for training physics teachers to use the materials. While not developed exactly according to accepted principles of systems design, it could be said that the Zacharieas group developed a system for teaching physics.

The foreign language field has recently contributed

some very systematic approaches to instruction. There is one system for teaching elementary French which consists of books, workbooks, tapes, records, and films. These materials can be supplied in a case with the necessary hardware. The films supplied, while in color, come in both 8mm and 16mm, and can be used on television.

Throughout the materials field, organized and semisystematic collections of instructional materials continue to make their appearance. Eight millimeter single concept films are being marketed in sets and are related to textual materials; even the textbook industry is publishing sets of books, workbooks, tests, and materials from which overhead transparencies can be copied. Some of the newer work, as, for example, by the AIBS (biology) group is even more systematic. Materials now being tested by this group lead the teacher almost step by step through the teaching process

It is, safe to say that this move toward organization and system in the instructional materials field is one of the most solid trends of the technological revolution in education. Its implication for the role of the teacher in the future, is, of course, tremendous. The systems approach to instruction also has a hardware aspect. Up to the present time this has shown up principally in an attempt to bridge the gap between the technology of mass instruction and the technology of individual instruction. In a sense the language laboratory has always done this, as the individual student in the laboratory deals with what is, in effect, a mass communication system.

However, there are several devices now being used that bridge this gap more directly. These devices provide for mass stimulus, but allow each individual student to react to what he sees by pressing a button, turning a dial, or otherwise informing the systems to his response.

These devices go under the general name of classroom communicators. One such device is now being used in several of the Job Corps camps. The data derived from the students response can be processed in several ways, for example, providing the teacher with an immediate read-out of how well the students are performing,. The materials for such a system have to be very carefully programmed and are, of course, highly systematic. This requirement is the biggest problem in connection with the use of this equipment.

There are several other ways to consider the systems approach to instruction For example, the small group interested in computer applications to education seems to take the position that the only systems approach to education through the computer. This will probably be the ultimate systems approach.

Organizational concepts

As was indicated by the introductory material, organization is a major aspect of technology. As might be expected, organization concepts better fitted to present educational needs are being suggested and applied. We are considering here only organization for instruction—not other proposals having to do with the governing and financing of the educational system as a whole. In essence, there are two such organizational patterns on the current scene which have many common aspects. The first, usually associated with the name of John Goodlad, reorganizes the elementary (and junior high) school into an ungraded pattern, permitting the individual student to progress much more easily at his own rate. The system of grade classes, imported from Germany in the 19th century, is unrealistic in the sense of human variability. It was, in its day, a technological solution to a chaotic problem. Whether the ungraded elementary school is the answer for 1965 yet remains to be seen. The requirements in terms of materials, individualized instruction and the like are frightening. The second new system of organization is applied to the secondary school and is usually referred to as the Trump Plan after the originator, Lloyd Trump. Trump has attempted to break up the "egg crate," 30-students-to-a-classroom situation in the high school and provide for large-group instruction (40 per cent), small seminar instruction (20 per cent), and individualized instruction (40 per cent). This concept is formally referred to as the Staff Utilization Plan. Inherent in this system is the idea of team teaching where teams of teachers, sometimes under a master teacher, manage these several responsibilities.

Various aspects of this plan have been tried out all over the United States, and the idea seems to be moving into practice. It should be emphasized that the Trump Plan is also postulated on a much wider use of instructional instrumentation than now exists, particularly for large-group and individualized instruction (Many existing team teaching experiments do not have this component).

Another aspect of the technological revolution in education is Curriculum reform. Reference was made above to the physical Science Study Committee. The PSSC set the Pattern for curriculum reform, backed by money from private foundations and the National Science Foundation. Since that time, following the PSSC pattern to some extent, in biology, chemistry, mathematics, and many other fields have been organized. As of two years ago, the NEA identified 37 such projects. Almost all of these have an orientation to instructional technology in some or all of its aspects—television, programmed instruction, films. In other words, the approach to the radical revision of the educational process is through the materials and devices of instruction.

The current situation in educational psychology

If the approach to change in education is viewed, at least in some quarters, through the materials and devices of instruction, it follows that the psychological orientation of these devices and materials within the teaching-learning process is of crucial importance. This is the area of applied educational psychology, or, as was indicated in a previous section, what some theorists, such as Lumsdaine and Glaser, consider to be the technology of instruction. The current situation, however, within educational psychology is, to say the least, mixed. Very few theorists or practitioners would be willing to say that one given point of view has achieved all of the answers. In the general practice of schoolkeeping today, an electric point of view as to theory coupled with a large portion of experience-passed-on-down constitutes the operational base.

Within the general literature of learning theory and related matters, there have been many attempts to distinguish, describe, even to reconcile various theories of learning. Hilgard, for example, in a classic work treats nine theories of learning. Such considerations are important to the scientist exploring this area, but it is highly likely that most practitioners today—teachers, materials producers, etc—could not make the sometimes subtle distinctions between these points of view, and certainly could not consciously apply these distinctions to real life problems of teaching and learning.

The uninitiated person reading only a portion of the literature might get the impression that the matters of teaching and learning were pretty well settled by the psychologists. This is not the case. However, since the educational process is ongoing and since children and adults come to school daily, some kind of commitment to a point of view is often made, particularly at the growing edge of educational technology. The following brief description of the situation must be read with this fact in mind and also remembering that most practice does not have a coherent theoretical base.

The most dominant point of view within the area of instructional technology today is that of Prof Jerome Bruner of Harvard. Professor Bruner's point of view has been adopted by the Zacharias group which began the national movement of curriculum revision through the materials and devices of instruction with the physics course of the Physical Science Study Committee. This group has extended its activities to such areas as elementary school science, and its point of view and methodology are, it is believed, dominant throughout almost all national efforts at curriculum revision, even including music and the fine arts.

At the great risk of oversimplification, Bruner and his colleagues, because they have carefully and brilliantly studied what is known as cognitive structure, have emphasized two general concepts:

1. Knowledge in a given field has a structure that can be taught and on which all individual facts and events can be hung.
2. Such a structure is best learned by the method of "discovery" or "inquiry", which in turn will help the learner be more creative and able to learn all his life.

Bruner's ideas have received great acceptance among scientists, mathematicians and, interestingly enough from many old-line progressive educators. A popular source for Bruner's ideas i his little book The Process of Education. His concern with other aspects of learning may be found in another small volume, On Knowing.

Again, recognizing the difficulties of oversimplification in a brief treatment such as this, B.F. Skinner, also of Harvard, can be thought of as holding a point of view almost directly opposite to that of Bruner. Skinner has recently criticized the Bruner position in a popular article and in a technical essay. Skinner, recognized as the father of teaching machines and programmed instruction in the modem sense, has a theory of teaching and learning known as operant conditioning in which the individual learner's behaviour is "shaped" by positive reinforcements administered under certain contingencies and following certain schedules. Theoretically, programmed instruction of the so-called linear type is designed to do this. In practice, very few programmers write programs according to pure Skinnerian principles. Skinner has had an enorrnous influence on the thinking of psychologists, and it is safe to say that most psychologists today are behaviourists who would be willing to accept a great deal, if not all, of Skinner's point of view. The fact remains, however, that his influence on educational practice, particularly on educational technology, as it is being applied, is small compared with that of Bruner.

A third point of view, for the moment somewhat outmoded, may be described as anti-technological and existential. It is stubbornly held, however, by a portion of the educational community, notably those most concerned with child development and the person, and some of those concerned with creativity. These latter often accept much of the Bruner position in addition. In some ways this position combines a little of the old gestalt concepts with the so-called assumptive view of perception and a great deal of emphasis upon self-actualization and self-perception. These concepts, combined with certain others derived from psychotherapy are often referred to today as "existential" psychology.

There are, of course, other theories of teaching and learning; the so-called neo-behaviourists, for example, adhere to a range of closely overlapping points of view. We are speaking here primarily of the views of practitioners (considered broadly) concerned with developing educational technology. In this connection, several newer positions which appear to have promise for or are related to instructional technology should be mentioned. Studies in neurophysiology have resulted in a theory of thought in behaviour; dealing with the electro-chemical functions of the central nervous system; memory has been studied with reference to changes in nervous structure, etc. Such a viewpoint is appealing to some theorists in instructional technology, probably because of its science-technology relationship.

Closely related to the interest in neuropsychology and even more closely related to developments in technology in general is what is often referred to as the cybernetic model of behaviour and learning. Essentially, this viewpoint undertakes to explain thought and behaviour in terms of models derived from the studies of computers. An excellent statement of this position may be found in Miller, Galanter and Pribham. In many ways, this theory can be considered an information theory of learning and is related to an even more elaborate concept—J.P. Guilford's structure of intellect. David Ausubel has recently published a theory relating only to what he calls "reception learning", or the processes of learning meaningful verbal materials, arguing that this type of teaching is, what is principally done in school . All of this work suggests that it will influence technological applications in education within the next decade. If this is true, some changes in current trends will occur.

Finally, it should be noted that both dominant and emerging, theoretical positions in the literature merely emphasize the fact that the educational practitioner cannot turn to a science of learning for his answers. This has resulted in a technological or empirical approach to solving practical problems of teaching and learning. This point of view is espoused by Ofiesh and is contained in Part II The empiricists hold that materials, devices and Processes must be validated in advance in terms of well-stated objectives of instruction on the students on which they are to be used. In other words, materials, devices and processes are produced on a best-guess basis, are tried out, are refined or changed as necessary, and are tested again. The process is repeated until a system that works is derived. Such a concept can be considered as a sheer technological or engineering approach and is so referred to by those who advocate it.

If present efforts at research, development and theory construction continue to expand; if, for example, the national research and development centers and the regional educational laboratories take root and grow; it can be expected that a much greater alignment of theory and practice of teaching and learning will come about within the next two decades. While it is unlikely that the answer will be achieved in this first new thrust, the move toward the classic relation of science to technology in the field of education will be speeded up.

Research and development

The history of research and development in the field of instructional technology is a long story in itself. Contributing to the quantum jump of 1958 in this field was the passage of Title VII of the National Defense Education Act. Title VII provided both for research in the new media field and for dissemination of information about new media to the educational community. Although the amounts of money available have been small (too small) the effect has been large. Psychologists and other educational research workers have turned their attention to educational media and fundamental questions concerning effectiveness and use of the technology of instruction have been investigated.

The Cooperative Research Group in the U.S. Office of Education has also fonded some studies in the field of instructional technology, and some research has been backed by other government agencies concerned with manpower retraining, etc Compared to the need, this research effort is still too small and the dissemination of the results of this research leaves much to be desired.

The new Elementary and Secondary Education Act of 1965 contains a provision of $ 45 million for what are known as regional educational laboratories. These laboratories (actually, they will probably be more like groups of cooperating institutions and school districts) are supposed to do research and then apply the results of this research to practice. The task force which worked preparing the background for the bill, had in mind something like Professor Zacharias' Educational Services Inc., a nonprint corporation which produces the materials for PSSC and other curriculum projects. However, it is likely that the organization of the laboratories will be much broader. There is no doubt, however, that there will be a large component of activity relating to instructional technology in these laboratories.

While many important research questions need to be settled, the great problem is the dissemination of the results of this work and the application of these findings to practice. To take just one example, there is very little evidence that research findings on programmed instruction have actually been applied in the construction of many programs that are available; further, the use of programmed instruction in the schools remains at a minimum level—the movement has not affected practice a great deal. The great foundations of this country have contributed both, to the research effort surrounding instructional technology in this decade and to the development work associated with it. Actually, foundation support has principally been for development and, as such, it has been more of an economic than an intellectual force. Because of this, it will be treated in the next section.

The infusion of capital

If technological capability—machines, materials, etc.—is viewed as capital, the educational system of this country is still poverty-ridden. Using hardware as a measure of this capability, Finn, Perrin and Campion found it to be relatively low. This low capital level is why, during this crucial decade of 1955 to 1964, foundation support has in many cases been decisive and has turned the path of American education into new, technological directions. The role of the Ford Foundation in this picture cannot be underestimated. Especially in the field of television, the support from the Ford Foundation was decisive. This included help for weak educational television stations, the establishment of the National Education Television Network Service, support for a national effort in instructional television, the institution of the airborne television program in the midwest, etc. Millions of dollars helped build technological capability and, of course, included other activities besides television; for example, the founding and support of the Educational Facilities Laboratories which are designed to improve educational construction of all kinds.

Other foundations, notably Carnegie, also contributed to this buildup. However, other than television, viewing the needs of the country as a whole, all the foundation money put together could only be described as seed corn. It remained for the U.S. Congress to provide funds for a much larger capital infusion into the American educational system.

From the point of view of educational technology, Title III of the National Defense Education Act made all the difference. In its original form, it provided money on a matching basis for states to furnish local school systems with funds to purchase materials and equipment for teaching science, mathematics and modern foreign languages. This provision has since been expanded to cover other areas of the curriculum. Under the older restrictions, approximately 60 to 70 per cent of the funds went into science equipment and the balance into audiovisual materials and equipment. These percentages are no doubt changing and, during the last year, the amount of money expended under the provisions of this title was about $ 90 million.

Almost all of the acts relating to manpower are designed to provide money for research and for teaching equipment and materials. No estimates were available to the writer as to the exact amount of such funds, but they are considerable and will contribute to the overall increase in technological capital for the educational system. Acts of the Congress relating to manpower were climaxed with the passage of the Economic Opportunity Act of 1964—the so-called War on Poverty. In the fact, provision is made for centers for the basic education and vocational training of jobless youths. In the organization and development of these centers, the assumption has been made that a great deal of use must be made of instructional technology because the system of instruction it is believed, must be considerably different from that used in schools from which these young people dropped out in the first place.

The latest act of Congress affecting instructional technology is the Elementary and Secondary Education

Act of 1965. Mention has already been made of the laboratory provision. One title of the act provides for the strengthening of library services, and this will add to the technological capital available to schools, as library services will include materials other than books. Another section provides for supplementary educational centers. These are conceived very broadly and will contain everything from guidance and remedial services to resident musicians. These centers will obviously have a media component and may end up as, among other things, regional centers for more sophisticated technological services. Plans for these program are just being laid.

There are other governmental influences in the field of instructional technology; for example, the wide use of many of these techniques in the training programs of the armed services. Accepting the fact that the American educational system remains primitive from the point of view of technological development, it is no different from other parts of the public sector, such as the field of social work. This concept, of course, can be traced to Galbraith who suggested in the Affluent Society that investment must move into the public sector and that we should treat such institutions as education' with at least as much generosity as we do Las Vegas or the Strategic Air Command.

In addition, the economics of the defense and space program cannot forever remain at the same levels. These programs have created great scientific—based industries with tremendous technical and manpower capabilities. Reduction in space and defense programs could cause social problems of no mean magnitude. It is no accident, therefore, that the Galbraithian concept of beefing up the public sector of the economy should be linked to the potentials of the aerospace, defense and science-related industries.

With some anticipation in the earlier manpower acts, this policy became reality when the Economic Opportunity Act of 1964 provided for the participation of industry in the Job Corps and other program. This put the science-related industries into the education business and, in the perspective of the general scientific-technological revolution, was inevitable anyway. Further, many of these industries or industrial groups had made previous passes at private educational developments and already had created some special educational capability.

The various acts discussed above provide a considerable amount of money and are an enticement for the science-based industries to enter the educational field. Since most of them have a quick-reacting capability, it was to be expected that the last few months have been occupied with tooling up, preparing proposals, reorganizing in the direction of what can only be called "educational diversification", and otherwise preparing to move into this new enterprise.

Several of the large Job Corps camps, as was indicated above, are being operated by these industries, sometimes in combination with a university. However, the most interesting signs are those related to mergers, acquisitions, joint venture agreements, and the like. Raytheon has purchased EDEX, a classroom communicator manufacturer, and Dage Television. Xerox has created a research laboratory in the basic behavioural sciences and has acquired Basic Systems and American Educational Publishers; Westinghouse has acquired the entire programming capability of Teaching Machines Inc.; Litton Industries and Hughes Aircraft have both built up in-house capabilities in these fields and, particularly in the case of an acquisition-oriented Company like Litton, acquisitions of various kinds may be expected.

These industrial groups are aggressive and have

access to highly educated manpower both in-house and on a consulting basis. The effect of these developments is not yet clear, but some of them ought to be pretty obvious. There is not too much manpower available in the instructional technology field, and hence, there will be competition for manpower. The very existence of technology-based instructional programs in Job Corps camps, etc., will put pressures on the schools. School board members may not be so reluctant to vote funds for instructional technology once the industrial factor becomes evident, and they may even put pressure on school administrators.

The preceding section covers the current situation with emphasis upon the decade 1955 to 1964, a crucial period for the development of educational technology. The changes occurring during this period were so striking that forecasting in this field appears extremely risky. Further, it cannot be overemphasized that developments involving any appreciable degree of novelty are still very slow to effect educational practice. In effect, events occur at two levels: An analogy might be to consider the interest in research and development now occurring in educational technology as the upper level of ocean currents which can be seen and measured, and actual practice in the majority of educational institutions and systems as the deep, slow-swelling, cold currents that move in their own time and are difficult to detect.

Nevertheless, there are probabilities and trends in the situation, and prediction is possible, although its accuracy cannot be stated even with the precision of probability statements now used in weather forecasting. What follows in this section is such a prediction; it is the sole responsibility of the author. For reasons which should become clear, this forecast is divided into two parts—a short-range forecast and a long-range forecast.

An analysis of the situation suggests that the next five to 10 years will be a period of consolidation and spread into educational practice of the technological developments of the last decade. The educational system has, in effect, been threatened with novelty, in the coming decade the novelty will be absorbed to the point where it will be no longer novel. There will be some new developments, these however, will tend W be in the political-social-economic sphere and not, as many of the current thinkers in educational technology suppose, in materials, hardware and psychological breakthroughs. Breakthroughs and novel developments are always possiblc these days, but the current trends continue to suggest that their time is, perhaps, a decade or more away. Based on the generalization that consolidation of gains will characterize the next decade, the following forecast is made from current trends:

1. *Innovation-change.* It has become the official policy of the U.S. Office of Education to encourage educational innovation; further the concept of innovation is "in" with the entire educational community at state, regional and local levels. Three forecasts can be made in this area:

    a. The principal site of education innovation will changc from the lower levels of the school system to higher education. Colleges and universities will be forced to innovate, principally due to the flood of students, but with other factors acting as an influence as well. Universities, while sources of innovation for the whole culture, have been loath to make drastic changes in their own procedures, particularly their teaching procedures. The innovations which will be forced on the higher educational system during the next decade will, therefore, cause a great deal of strain.

b. With respect to the system as a whole particularly the public school system—educational innovation will become institutionalized, centering upon the U.S. Office of Education and, secondarily, the several state departments of education. Existing legislation and plans and the influence of a new educational establishment will all combine to push this now visible trend into actuality.

The principal instruments for this institutionalization are likely to be the regional laboratories now being set up by the U.S. Office of Education together with regional educational centers to be set up under Title III of the Elementary and Secondary Education Act of 1965. However, even if these instruments are not used for one reason or another, others will be found, and the innovative process will be institutionalized.

With the institutionalization of educational innovation; two things will happen. First, the innovations themselves' as they are picked up by units of the system will become simplified and vulgarized, sometimes beyond recognition, and will lose a great deal of their power. This is principally due to the fact that the system as a whole is not sophisticated enough to absorb many of the new processes and procedures with all of their subtleties and qualifications.

Secondly and more important, as the process of innovation is institutio-nalized, innovation will gradually become little more than change. This is based on the assumption that the "innovation of the method of invention" as applied to educational innovation and that is the avowed purpose of this institutionalization will not necessarily work with the same force that it has with industrial technology. It is likely that the true innovators will begin to drop out of such an institutionalized system, and the remaining bureaucracy will not be capable of far-reaching innovation.

2. The Development of the New Educational Establishment. American education has always seemed to have more common procedures, goals and even buildings and teaching materials than are warranted by existence of 50 autonomous and presumably different state school systems..

There are many reasons for this, but among those often, cited is the existence of an educational establishment. In the past, it has been stated that this establishment has consisted of the national educational associations, the teachers colleges and schools of education in universities, and the state departments of education. After 1950, this establishment came under heavy fire, and beginning about 1955, a new educational establishment began to emerge. The significance of this new educational establishment for this paper is that it has a scientific-technological base. Essentially, it consists of four or five of the leading higher institutions in the United States, several foundations, a component of the new scientist-politicians that have emerged in the last 20 years, and some able individuals both within and without government. Its relation to the older establishments is almost nil.

The next decade will see the complete domination of educational thinking in this country by this new establishment as it develops and consolidates. Nothing in this statement should be construed as suggesting that there is anything conspirational about this emergence. It is doubtful, for example, whether individuals now belonging to the new establishment even know it as such. Rather, the emergence of such a group of intellectual leaders for education was almost foreordained by the development of our advanced technological society.

Henceforth, the new establishment will orient American education more in the direction of science and technology as associated with its own processes and will absorb only that part of the older establishment which will fit this overall scientific-technological pattern.

3. *The Systemization of the Materials of Instruction.* The already well-developed trend toward more systematic organization of instructional materials will reach fruition in application in schools and colleges within the next few years. Systems of teaching the structure of subject matter and certain skills such as reading will be applied on an increasing scale. These systems will make use of all of the available instructional technology and will absolutely control the curriculum in the areas systems will be created, and schools and colleges will be asked to choose among systems; however, since these systems are expensive and take years to develop, the choices will be limited Further, there, will be problems of obsolescence and logistics associated with them for which the schools and colleges are ill prepared.

The materials within these systems will increasingly be tailored directly to learning tasks and will represent much more of a rifle approach than the historic shotgun approach of the standard textbook or educational film. As such, their overall effect should be more efficient. Further, research now going on in several places should have begun to supply some answers to the general question as to which medium is the most effective for a given purpose. If these answers do develop, the emerging instructional systems will also reflect this knowledge. Increasingly large amounts of money will be spent on developing these systems.

4. *Developments in Hardware.* Hardware, particularly in

sophisticated systems, such as military weapons systems, can change or develop rapidly. On the other hand, in the consumer field, such as refrigerators and automobiles, the changes tend to be slower and are often more apparent than real. In the field of instructional technology both possibilities are present.

a. *Optical-photographic versus electronic systems.* Because of the long lead time that Optical-photographic (conventional audiovisual) systems (projectors, film, etc.) have had on electronic systems (television, videotape, etc.), existing instructional hardware is heavily weighted toward the optical-photographic for pictorial (and audio) storage and transmission. Further, photographic information is still superior to electronic by a factor of, perhaps 100:1. There are other influences as well, such as accessibility.

The next few years will see a continuing invasion of this field by electronic transmission. Improvements will be made in the information capabilities of electronic systems; the transmission of color will become cheaper and easier; accessibility will be improved through cheaper videotape-type storage; and videotape recorders and players win become smaller, less expensive, and easier to operate with reliability. By the end of the decade, a new balance will have been achieved between these two (partially) competing systems. Neither will disappear, but electronic and optical-photographic systems will claim a much greater share of existing hardware designed for pictorial storage and transmission than is the case now.

b. *Television, videotape, etc.* As indicated above, videotape players and recorders will become smaller, cheaper and more reliable. Whether the current methods of recording on magnetic tape will still be in use might be in question, as there are several other ways to use electronic impulses to record information on some medium; thermoplastic recording is an example. The precise means is unimportant from the educational point of view. What this does mean is that images and sound will be available inexpensive, easy-to-use form.

In addition, it is to be expected that television will expand in its educational aspects during the same period of time. This expansion will principally be in the closed-circuit and 2,500mg areas and not in broadcast television for schools and colleges. The expansion will occur first in higher education, and it can be fairly confidently predicted that inter-institutional cooperation in the use of television, such has been experimented with in Oregon, will be extended as the pressures on higher education increase. A professor in one institution teaching a class in another, or several others, will not be at all unique except in small enrolment, prestige institutions. Even in such cases, lectures from Nobel Prize winners and the like will probably be delivered by television.

Along with these developments in television and, for a while at least overshadowing them, will be an enormous increase in the use of telephone lines to transmit certain kinds of educational materials. The last few years, have seen some growth in the so-called 'teleculture" technique where the lecturer at one location can speak to a group via amplified telephone at some other location. Recently, as at the Harvard Business School and in connection with various medical education projects conference-type seminars between groups have been held using the telephone system. A new invention makes it possible for a teacher to draw while lecturing over the telephone and have the image projected by a special overhead projector at the receiving end; slides and other materials distributed in advance have also been successfully used with telecultures. Since this procedure is relatively inexpensive and very useful, it may be expected to grow spectacularly during the decade.

c. *Other hardware developments.* While improvements and changes may be expected in all audiovisual equipment, it is likely that the major advances will occur in the field of self-instructional devices. There are, at present several prototypes under development of multimedia machines designed as individual instruction devices. While the history of this type of teaching machine has not been too spectacular up to this point, it seems reasonable to predict that the next decade will find several types of these in use. This, of course, will set a new requirement for programming and production of materials.

The 8mm film, particularly with the new format, will constitute the most important development in the audiovisual field in the next few years. Following Professor Forsdale of Teachers College, it is believed that 8mm will be used primarily for individual instruction, although with the new format classroom projectors for groups of up to 50 in size may be expected to become quite common. As 8mm comes in a technological lag problem will become apparent with the huge investment the educational system has in 16mm film and projectors. One way around this problem will be to develop individual instruction devices for use with 8mm film, particularly devices that permit student response. Considerable resistance to this development may be expected. Multi-media/multi-screen techniques for large groups will continue to expand during the next 10 years. Lecture halls and briefing rooms will be built with such hardware requirements in mind. Automatic projection equipment will be redesigned in order to operate in gangs for this purpose, and control equipment will be developed on a miniaturized, high reliability form.

d. Computers and the interface problem. Since a separate paper has been prepared on computer applications to education, computers for computer-based instruction will not be discussed here. However, it may be important to point out or re-emphasize that there are certain needed hardware developments related to computer-based instruction which will probably occur during the decade under consideration. These developments are referred to as the interface between the computer and the student and have been the subject of a recent study by Glaser, Ramage and Lipson. In the next 10 years various ingenious interface devices will be developed so that students may receive stimulation in various forms form a computer (pictures, words, numbers, sounds, graphs), many manipulate the subject matter so presented with instruments such as fight pens, and may be informed on other portions of the interface device as to progress, what to do next, etc. Until such interface devices are developed, computer-based instruction will never achieve its full potential.

Essentially, at least a portion of what should go into such an interface device is the result of developments which, in the computer field, go under the, general name of information display. Although the existing literature seems to suggest it, there is nothing in the educational picture which would require all such display techniques to be confined to devices requiring student response and controlling student behaviour in detail. It is reasonable, in fact, to predict that information display techniques which are essentially electronic or electronic-optical in character will also be used in connection with television, other wave-propagated transmission and telephone to convey teaching materials from one point to another without elaborate response and measuring devices. As yet, with the exception of a few experiments, the techniques of information display in use with sophisticated systems, such as space and space support systems, have not been tried with education problems. The next decade will see many developments in this area, including stimulation.

5. Information Storage and Retrieval. An area which may develop as spectacularly in the next 10 years as the language Laboratory and associated teaching techniques did in the 1955 to 1964 decade is the area of information storage and retrieval. As such, in its educational applications, it could represent an exception to the general orientation of this section.

The problem of the information explosion is well known; the fact that much information today never reaches & book stage in time but remains in the form of documents, articles, et has given rise to a whole new profession known as "documentalists"—experts in information storage and retrieval are calling themselves, "information scientists—and there are signs within the old-line professional library field of a deep schism between conventional librarians and information scientists and documentalists.

Obviously, new technological information storage and retrieval techniques can be applied to he problems of a conventional library. However, except for large university libraries, it does not seem likely that these techniques will make much of an inroad into school and college libraries during the next decade.

What is likely to happen is that sort of an end run will occur, and the new technology of information storage and retrieval will reach the educational system in some strength outside of the main library stream. There are several reasons for this. Again, the position of the U.S. Office of Education may be crucial; however, it is the considered opinion of the writer that even if that office were not a factor, this phenomenon would occur. Operating from a center in Washington, D.C., and from, perhaps, up to 200 satellites or clearinghouses located in higher institutions and research centers, of various types, microfiche chips containing research documents will be supplied educational users ordering from a system of indexes, bibliographies and abstracts also provided by ERIC. This system is now underway on a small scale.

The availability of this information will create a demand for microfilm readers of various types and for equipment to reproduce hardcopy from microfilm. Such readers are all with some modification—potential teaching machines; further, the ability to reproduce hardcopy presents the possibility of expanding such services to instructional materials too current to be available in any other form. Such a procedure has been experimented with in San Diego County, California, for some years with great success, where local industries and scientific institutions have been where local industries and scientific institutions have been supplying schools with current scientific materials produced in this way.

If this development proceeds as suggested—and the probabilities are high—a full-fledged educational information storage and retrieval system may grow up outside existing channels. Further, because the hardware and services are adaptable, it is possible that a new generation of teaching machines will come into being based on the microfiche reader, thus short-circuiting a whole series of obstacles. The presence of hardcopy-producing equipment might speed up the use and adaptation of newer curriculum materials both in programmed and in more conventional forms. Such a development would tend to restore a certain amount of curriculum independence to local school districts, providing staff and facilities were made available to take advantage of it. This latter development is highly unlikely. What is more likely is, as the state departments become stronger, curriculum materials will be supplied by the state departments in this easier-to-use form and curricular autonomy will be lost, not gained, at the school and district level.

6. *Standardization*. One of the strongest trends in the next decade will be a general more toward standardization, a move inevitable in any highly technical society. With respect to equipment and materials, several forces are at work that potentially, could force standardization. The first of these is the so-called "state plan" by which many of the federal educational program dispense money to the states. In its most simplified form, the state submits plan for a program, for example, dispensing funds under Title III or the National Defense Education Act. Once this plan has been approved, the state, in effect, sites in control of the disbursement of the finds to its local and regional units. All the state has to do is to require standards for equipment in its plan and standardization becomes a reality. With the so-called "Compact of States" within the immediate future, providing for efficient communication between the states on educational matters, standardization could soon become national.

A second force, which has been discussed for many years but has never been released, is possible if the major cities of the United States were to combine in order to write common specifications for equipment and materials. Such cities represent a large share of the market and now contribute to the chaos in educational equipment standards by requiring annoying and, most often, useless differences in specifications. This raises the price per unit on such items as projectors, complicates bidding procedures, and localizes purchases. Economic considerations may force the end of this practice and a move to joint bidding or even centralized purchasing. Such a possibility is only a possibility and it is more likely that the provincial practice, of the educational bureaucracies of such mammoth systems as New York and Los Angeles will remain at the level of their archaic city building codes. Of the two forces, the state force, even including centralized purchasing, will probably prevail, and equipment and, to a certain extent, materials standardization will occur during the decade under discussion.

At a broader level, greater standardization will be forced on the present quasi-autonomous school system than now exists through such factors as the increasing influence of federal educational programs, even if no direct control is sought or applied the inevitable cooperation of states and regions in educational matters; the introduction of whole systems of instruction; the possibility of a national assessment program; the reduction in the number of educational materials suppliers; the reduction in the total number of school districts in the United States; the general increase of communication; the prevalance of a large scale industrial thinking as it moves into the public sector; and the move toward computer data control.

7. *The National Assessment (Testing) Program.* Earlier in this paper it was mentioned that testing had been developed over the past several decades into a formidable subtechnology within the broader field of

educational technology. The influence of the New York Regents Examinations upon the curriculum of the schools in New York State has been commented upon for many years. Recently, this type of influence has extended throughout the nation with the examinations of the College Entrance Examination Board, the National Merit Scholarship Examinations, the Graduate Record Examination, etc. Attention here is devoted to examinations that affect the curriculum of the schools and not to other forms of testing, such as psychological and attitude.

The next decade will see the institution of some form of national education assessment program. The word assessment is used advisedly because the sponsors of the idea are proposing to combine standard achievements testing techniques with sampling techniques similar to those used in public opinion polls to assess "how well the schools are doing'. Such a program would not be achievement testing in the accepted sense. Once such an assessment program is underway, it will become another powerful force for standardization The technical capability already exists. Current moves underway to make this capability operational by taking the necessary political, social, and economic steps will no doubt be successful. The claims already being made that such a program will not force a certain amount of standardization are rejected by the writer. That is not the issue anyway. The questions that remain to be answered are what kind of standardization and whether or not the standardization so created *will* be good or bad.

8. *Trends in Administration.* Many trends in the field of school and college administration could be singled out for projection. For example, at the brick-and-mortar level, school buildings will continue to improve and be made more compatible with the

existing and developing instructional technology. Of all possible predications in the field of administration, four are selected for comment.

The first, discussed at length in Mr. Bushnell's paper, will only be mentioned briefly. Data-processing equipment and computers will become common tools for the school ad administrator in handling many routine problems; better decisions will be possible because of the immediate availability of better data. Centralized data-gathering centers will appear, probably as regional centers within the several states. Later, and inevitably, these will be joined into some kind of national network.

Secondly, the most important function to be developed during the next decade will be a logistics of instruction. Everything within the new instructional technology—systems, complex use of materials, sophisticated equipment, new patterns of organization and buildings—requires formidable logistical support. The whole system will break down without it. Such support involves planning based on precise objectives and data, materials flow, equipment maintenance and replacement, backup manpower to the teacher, etc. Such thinking at present is almost completely foreign to school administrators at all levels except in a primitive form that provides sufficient pencils and sweeping compound for the year. Logistical thinking has rarely been applied to instruction; first, therefore, a theory of instructional logistics will have to be created. The pressures of the developing instructional technology will force it into being within the decade.

The third projection is somewhat broader than the first two but is related to them. Essentially, it is that organization patterns will move into larger and larger units for administrative purposes and that control will become more and more a part of what is sometimes called a corporate structure. In other words the educational bureaucracy will enlarge, with an effort to make the parts interchangeable.

The precise pattern of the enlarging units may take several forms during the decade ahead. The main point is that there will be an increase in size, which, of course, will in turn increase the distance between the top levels and the point of contact with students. All state systems of education will tend to become real systems instead of the semisystems now existing. The regional laboratories, the Compact of States, and other such developments mentioned above, when combined with state plans, school district consolidation, and urban growth are all forces operating in this situation. It is hard to see anything but a diminution of local control of schools in the next 10 years. This diminution will tend to accelerate toward the end of the decade.

Finally, it is probable that one or more new private school systems, national in scope, will be started during this same period. These systems will be developed by the new industries moving into the educational field and will feature highly standardized, relatively fully automated, high-quality education designed essentially for upper— and upper middle-class clientele. Sich a system or systems will be accompanied by, but probably not related to, similar systems of private vocational training centers. This movement, too, will be gaining impetus by the end of the decade.

The school administrator required by these and many will quite-clearly be a skilled *professional manager,* not the Latin scholar or part-time chemist-administrator, as desirable as such characteristics seem to many people; and he will not be so much the community-oriented, faithful service club member so highly valued in some school administration circles today. Subject matter scholars, through the technique of curriculum development projects, have learned to short-circuit school boards and administrators in matters of curriculum content. Increasingly, as methodology becomes more precise within educational technology, the same effect will be achieved by psychologists and educational engineers; thus, the issue of the ideal subject matter expert or liberal arts generalist qua school administrator will become completely dead, remaining to be mourned in the columns of literary magazines. The concept of the successful community-oriented administrator will also die, although a little more slowly, and the mourning will be heard at the annual steak fry.

9. *The Research, Development, Dissemination, and Adoption Syndrome and the Resistance to Innovation.* As the process of research, development, dissemination, and adoption begins to operate with force, the traditional resistance of the educational system to change will crumble at an increasing rate during the next 10 years.

Some enthusiasts for educational technology of any variety have consistently underestimated the power of the resistance of the system in the past; in the future, however, the timespan between idea and practice will increasingly be shortened. The current timespan between the development of a new process and its adoption by a substantial majority of units of the system has been estimated at about 35 years. During the next 10 years this timespan will be reduced to about one-quarter of that length, or from eight to 10 years.

10. *General Developments in Educational Psychology and Methodology.* Barring unexpected breakthroughs in understanding the physics and chemistry of the central nervous system which are, of course, possible, the situation in educational psychology as

described above will not change much during the decade Cognitive structure, inquiry, structure of knowledge, creativity, and student-response manipulation will still be key concepts both for pure and applied research and for the development and testing of instrumentation and materials. Increasingly, a dialog may be expected to develop between the cognitive structure inquiry school and the operant conditioning school; a hard core of each will hold firm, but borders will become increasingly friendly. Experiments attempting to turn one system into another, as, for example, that recently reported by·Schrag and Holland, will increase.

In the meantime, newer viewpoints, particularly those associated with cybernetic principles and information theory, win begin to gain momentum. A recent book by Smith and Smith may be a bellwether. Research patterns using these developing theories will begin to intrigue younger psychologists. The decade will end with some newer points of view having enough adherents to threaten what will then be "old hat" Psychology. Because the psychological situation will remain unsettled, the educational engineers will build bridges of learning on an empirical basis. The decade will see a great commitment to the empirical approach in the production of instructional materials and hardware. Materials and processes will be tested increasingly on suitable populations and will be revised until they work. The engineers, of course, will use whatever can be used from the studies of the pure psychologists; further, more research will be based on realistic student populations rather than small laboratory situations from which it is difficult to generalize.

The combination of the empirical approach and increased pure and applied research throughout the whole field of education and educational psychology represents one force that will turn a current form of thinking completely around so that it will point in the opposite direction.

The second force in operation relates to the national commitment to education as the uplifting force in our national life. For example, developing learning programs for such things as Operation Headstart and the Job Corps training centers are very difficult technical problems; they require, for their solution, large dozes of educational technology considered broadly—methods, processes, machines, organization, skilled specialist manpower. Pious claims to the contrary, a knowledge of subject matter alone win be of little or no help in dealing with a 16-year old illiterate from the Kentucky hills.

These two forces will combine into a pressure that will result in the rediscovery of educational methodology. From about 1950 to 1960 it was extremely fashionable to decry educational methodology as useless, as a fake machine sold by charlatans, as something certainly not needed in the process of instruction. Those that grudgingly conceded that methodology did exist equated it with "tricks of the trade"—something that could be picked up overnight on an apprentice basis.

An illustrative example relates to the problems which led to the creation of operation Headstart, a huge national operation designed to provide missing background for young, deprived children so that they might be ready to learn in school. It is now ironically forgotten that many critical books and articles appearing from 1950 to 1960 claimed that there was no such thing as "readiness" for learning and that professional educators, in maintaining that there was, were perpetrating a fraud on the American public. These books were read by the upper-level economic group and the articles appeared in the "best" magazines. The general downgrading of methodological concepts which resulted in its own methodology, is being attacked by events and will result in a complete destruction of this posture. Further, since control of subject matter is now secure through the technology of instructional systems, the entire dialog between method and subject matter will be wiped out.

11. *The Buildup of the New Educational Industry.* As was indicated earlier in this memorandum, one trend of the last decade was the emergence of the science-based industries into the educational scene. The result of this in the next decade will be a pattern of power struggle, mergers, acquisitions, and new combinations, such as joint ventures between such industries, universities and nonprofit corporations of the "think-tank" variety.

It is hard to see how the old-line publishing firms and audiovisual producers and suppliers can retain their current organization, appearance and way of doing business. The next 10 years will, see enormous changes in the educational business, which will generally be in the direction of larger, more diversified enterprises that will absorb many of the smaller companies and will force others out of business. The time of the lone salesman working out of his house for the small company and calling on a friendly territory will run out in this decade. The existence of this larger educational industry will gradually force a change in bidding and purchasing procedures, and hence, will influence the formation of the logistics of instruction. Such an industry will also permit more communication between the training segment and the pure educational segment because materials and equipment will be supplied to both. If the pattern continues in the direction it seems to be going at the present time, these industrial giants will, through contracts, also be operating educational enterprises. The current operation of some of the Job Corps training centers by industrial groups and nonprofit corporations will be followed by the development of a general contracting capability under which such companies will provide instructional materials and services, build buildings, process data, catalog books, and even hire or provide teachers and administrators for schools and colleges. Some of them may well develop their own school systems

Education to be relevant has to meet four criteria which are crucial for living in our modem, technologically advanced and complicated world.

1. First, education must be relevant to the world of work. Everyone going to school should be getting a wide range of vocational choices in how to earn a living. Students should not be prepared for a job but for a choice of jobs.
2. Education must be relevant to the political structure. A complicated society requires more understanding in legislative, executive and judicial decision making. This means student government has to be real to serve a real function.
3. A relevant education requires much more intellectual inquiry; people have to be turned on intellectually. It's not enough for people to do what a computer does better—code, store and retrieve facts. These, people must be able to fret and to conceptualize, they have to be able to analyze; they have to be turned on to literature, art, music, science, and maths. They have to become cultural carriers and they have to appreciate the various different cultures that a complicated society has.
4. International relations must be a part of a relevant education. People must acquire the competence to live with their neighbours in a more crowded society.

Unless education deals with the central issues of our time, the program is worthless. Education that is noncontroversial is meaningless. A scholar must do more than acquire a vocabulary; he must be involved in action. There is one point in education that must be non-negotiable. That point involves the Bill of Rights, the rights of an individual in a free society. Many schools work for behaviour modification—to get children to act alike and to look and dress alike. School administrators are very anti-Bill of Rights in this sense. Their system is very central—shape up or ship out. Media people who work with administrators must become passionate advocates of democracy. With complacency, a person becomes the enemy of democracy.

Two observations can be made about the education you people receive in our colleges today.

First, students end up hating books. They acquire this hatred systematically. You can't learn to enjoy reading if you have to pull something out of every book you pick up—if you have to produce a paper or a seminar report. This explains the attraction of university undergraduates to Marshall McLuhan. McLuhan has a philosophy that is basically anti-book and it's very attractive to people who come in contact with books the way university students do. The resaon there are underground books at a university is not that these books have more to say, but that students can read them without compulsion. You destroy a book by turning it into an assignment; you can destroy anything that way.

Second, university students are removed from men with ideas. Universities, are inhospitable to learned man—a man with a vision of unified knowledge. It is impossible for him to be a in a university because he isn't a good enough specialist. The university student comes in contact with intellectual technicians who are uninspiring and dull. No student can have any respect for them. A student cannot know what the life of the mind is like because he hates books and because he never comes in contact with men who have lived the life of the mind.

What are my suggestions to you about the direction of the education industry dialog, and I emphasize that we, the educators, are the ones that need to give this dialog direction? I would like to suggest some margins because I believe the marginal media man is always between this and that.

As a past supporter of behaviourism and shaping, I do not believe we should throw out the baby with the bath; but somehow we have got to get over on the human free side as well. We are sort of standing with one foot in both camps.

There are several things we need to do and I want conclude my speech with five suggestions:

1. We must alter our theoretical framework which is now moving in the direction of behavioural shaping at too rapid a rate. We must slow down this trend, though I don't mean to imply that we should wipe it out.

2. We have to consider the intellectual disciplines and begin a dialog with the people in there disciplines in order to help them make their teaching at all levels more relevant. I do not believe it is the content that ever was irrelevant—some of the things in Greek history are relevant to our current period—but the disciplinarians do not understand this. And I believe you can get them to understand, if you can get them to give more attention to the human factors involved.

3. 1 believe we should insist that the products and efforts of industry concentrate on the human being. In

the next few year we need more to follow the lead of Carl Rogers and Abraham Maslow than we do B.F. Skinner and other behaviourist,. With media and a different instructional design, we can move into the affective domain and be concerned with human beings.

4. We must also realize the need to effectively deal with power groups. I predict that we are going to have more conflict with teacher militancy, negotiations are going to hinge eventually on the application of educational technology whether money is to be spent on a language laboratory or to raise teachers' salaries. We have to deal with other minority and power groups as well. These groups include women and students, two of the most downtrodden minorities of our times. We must fight against any form of censorship whatsoever. I would make this absolute. If you sit once again like you did in the early 1950s, we will go down the tubes, I think, for sure. We must move to a general freedom, to openness, and be problem oriented in what we do and how we deal with people. We have got to encourage creativity, and this requires a different kind of medium from one designed for behavioural shaping.

5. Finally, I think we have to take a general ethical position. The question is very simple: Whose side are you going to be on? I don't mean to imply that industry is bad. And 1 claim no conspiracy theory. But isn't it time to give industry some direction? If no direction is given, it is inevitable that technology will take off on its own. We will have lost a battle and a war, a war that can be won very easily if you leave Okoboji with the determination to be on the side of human beings and the Bill of Rights no matter what.

Insitutionalization of Evaluation

We live in an age of analysis We also tend to synthesize and systematize everything we analyze in order to solve problems. These processes of analysis, synthesis and systematization are some of the power tools of our high-order scientific-technological society, aided, of course, by Such things as computers and punched cards which supply data about our bill-paying habits, our blood types, and our penchants for blondes, brunettes or redheads.

At the moment, the concern of the study group to which this paper is addressed is evaluation; not mere or abstract evaluation, but evaluation of the successes, failures, feasibilities and nonfeasibilities of various Title III innovative projects set up in school systems throughout the United States. Funds for this effort are supplied by the United States Congress and the projects are administered by the U.S. Office of Education, monitored by the several state departments of education, and worried about by local school administrators.

This interest in evaluation, in my opinion, must be seen in a technical-social-political context within the entire educational enterprise. The age of analysis in which we live is generating an age of assessment in education. Thus, we have a campaign developing for a national assessment program; several states are also asking and answering the same question within their borders. Other considerations aside, it would be no surprise, therefore, to see this evaluation zeitgeist penetrating the Title III program. How well are all of these Title III projects doing?

Further, as technological patterns of thinking and processing invade the previously primitive educational culture, it is inevitable that a drive for systematization should begin. For example, Hammond opens his paper on evaluation with the statement, "The need for a systematic approach to the evaluation of innovations has become one of education's most pressing problems" Analysis of a sophisticated variety must precede systematization, and such analyses can be found not only in Hammond but in Clark and Guba and Shufflebeam to refer to some very recent examples. It should be noted that all of the work cited is exceptionally rigorous and highly sophisticated. It provides an excellent base from which to attack certain practical evaluation problems, not only for Title III projects but for any instructional process; this work is in the high technical tradition and, as such, is relatively new to professional education.

Further, another sign of the analysis-synthesis-system approach to evaluation in education is the continual invention, development and refinement of instruments for use in evaluation processes. Test-makers are everywhere, inventing measuring devices ranging from pencil and paper tests to stimulators. Guba suggests many new measuring and feedback instruments are needed.

The general objective, then, seems to be in the direction of systemization of evaluation procedures. Sharp analyses, increasing and better instrumentation, process studies are all leading to Dr. Hammond's "systematic approach", to evaluation in general, and, if this study committee is any indication, to a systematic approach to evaluation for Title III projects. Such a movement to system should lead to a great deal of improvement.

I would like to point out however, that this movement toward system in evaluation also may not lead to improvement. For, in order for an evaluation system to be applied across the country, it is necessary first to institutionalize it; this is to say that, unless other means are invented, the evaluation system must be initiated, monitored and controlled by a bureaucratic system. Institutionalization of the evaluation process could destroy the innovative possibilities of Title III.

There is nothing inevitable in this potential destruction of the innovative process by the technical organization for evaluation. However, if the evaluation processes as institutionalized are not to be made into a missile system aimed at the heart of educational innovation, additional analysis and invention is absolutely necessary. The remainder of this paper will examine this problem and, in addition, report some observations on the evaluation provisions of a number of Title III proposals which were studied in some detail; hopefully, the problem examination and the proposal examination can be tied together to develop some recommendations to close the paper.

Why Evaluation Anyway?

The basic question that needs to be asked to begin this analysis is: Why is evaluation important in the educational enterprise? There are at least five purposes or reasons that can be presented in answer to this question:

1. To add to the substantive knowledge of educational processes.
2. To provide information in order to adjust, discard or otherwise change the application of an ongoing educational process.
3. To provide justification for a political-social-economic action relating to education.
4. To create a product which can move through educational bureaucratic systems and thus keep these systems operative.
5. To provide instruments which may be used to carry information on the success of the process to the educational community.

These five purposes do not' necessarily operate in a discrete fashion: in other words, in any one situation several may appear in the form of a mix. It is fairly easy, however, to identify the emphasis in each case. The five purposes will be briefly discussed in the paragraphs that follow.

The distinction between the first and second has been noted by many of the recent analysts, such as Shufflebeam and Guba. The first—measurements conducted under carefully controlled conditions—theoretically provides material for the corpus of educational research; as such, the results should add to the substantive understanding of educational processes. And, as has been pointed out many times, such results are rarely directly applicable to the problems of the practitioner and are of little use to decision makers. It is possible, however, for such product-oriented research to come into existence as a fallout or by-product of a much more comprehensive evaluation procedure. The use of such research techniques as the only means of approaching evaluation has been amply criticized in recent years.

The second purpose for evaluation is now thought to be the most important when examining ongoing innovative projects in education, such as those set up under Title 111. Here the decision maker gets information on a feedback system which tells him how well the process is going, what changes need to be made, etc. Various models of this evaluation procedure have been proposed.

This feedback evaluation system, designed to aid decision makers dealing with practical educational problems, such as the operation of a Title III innovative center, has not yet been criticized to any extent due to its novelty for the field of education and the careful construction of the emerging theoretical models.

However, the feedback evaluation system is open to criticism. It assumes, at the outset, that the decision-making process in a given school, school system, or other educational entity is rational. It is not, The folklore of education is *filled with* examples of the school business manager selecting curricular materials, the high school dean of women throwing Salinger out of the library, and others too numerous to mention. Prior questions have to be asked whenever the feedback evaluation system is proposed Who or what group is the decision maker? How does the power structure really work? What are the innovations? Unless these questions are answered and the rationality or irrationality of the particular system is analysed, the beautiful, precise and rational models of the feedback evaluation system will not work—or, at the very least, work very imperfectly.

The third purpose for evaluation is the purpose of justification. In this case, a board of education, a state legislature, a committee of Congress, or numerous other bodies both public and private need information in order to take some action respecting education. This action may be in appropriating funds hiring additional remedial reading teachers, purchasing a language laboratory, etc. Or, in the opposite case, it may be to fire the superintendent, set the building program back two years or reduce the audiovisual appropriation by 40 per cent, These actions *are justified by* evaluation, whether formal or informal. 'In the case of the disposal of school personnel, the evaluation before action may be choleric and personal; increasingly, however, as statistics become everyday playthings of the mass media, justifications for political-economic-social educational action are couched in, scientific garb, whether really scientific or not, We are all familiar with arguments which press in opposite directions for action by some public body based on the same evaluative report.

While it is obvious that public bodies with the appropriate authority over education have every right to evaluate information and, in fact, often need more than they get, it is equally true that the development of justification ought to be a secondary objective of educational evaluations carried out by professionals. This, of course, is a value judgement. It can be argued, for example, that the effort expended in developing a particular kind of justification evaluation in order to save a program known to be good is more important in the real world of politics that more technically adequate professional evaluation. The answer to this problem, it seems, is to pay attention to the two element, in the old cliche about the tail and the dog. An evaluation program set up only for justification purposes is unprofessional; a professional evaluation procedure on a program that is demonstrably good ought to develop sufficient data to justify its continuance or expansion.

2
Educational Media

Educators long have sought ways to adapt group methods of instruction in such ways that all children in the group progress at acceptable rates and reach satisfactory levels of achievement in reasonable amounts of time. It is not surprising that group teaching methods with some fixed set of materials normally fail to achieve the purpose. In both research and classroom practice, the attempt to find ways to meet individual needs by group methods tends to encounter confusion of three important parts of the problem; (a) criteria—how fast and how well the learner progresses; (b) the learning variables—why the child progresses or does not progress; and (c) the choice among methods for attempting to adapt group teaching to individual needs—branching instruction, parallel sets of material, grouping by ability, or diagnostic testing and remedial instruction.

If, somehow, attention could be focused first on the learning variables—why the person does not meet the criteria of progress—then insights might be gained into what the individual learner needs by way of instructional materials or media. We could then consider how this need can be met in spite of the necessity for group instruction. It is thus working backwards to ask first whether one should prefer to use ability grouping or branching programs, because one cannot know whether a branching program is the proper method for adapting to individual needs before he knows what the individual needs are. Branching is not the way to meet the need for example, if the branching is a branching by words when the learner needs a picture.

Therefore, no solutions will be found for method of making group-presented media fill individual needs because we are still uncertain as to the needs of the learner. Various lines of research endeavor, however, conducted by group experiments, do throw some light on the Problem. Interestingly enough, it is research with groups, using samples of actual instructional materials, which helps more than the individual treatments applied to one "subject" at a time in the learning laboratory. Apparently the variables used there are not the ones needed to solve the problem. More often than not, as will be seen, this group research employed programmed instruction as the medium for research.

While no one learning variable can yet be said to outweigh all others in importance, the following issues do seem worthy of exploration when searching for the key characteristics of media and materials which may eventually bring about effective individual learning in either individual or group situations: sensory mode; IQ; special aptitudes; entering competencies; sequencing of instruction; and programming variable" such as size of step, frequency of feedback, and variety of examples.

When more research has succeeded in identifying more fully the needs for learning by the individual, then progress later may be made in methods for adapting group media to individual needs in order to achieve the criteria. Is such continued research succeeds in identifying the kind of program the individual learner needs then it, may be possible at some point in the future to employ computers for highly successful branching instruction but probably not until then.

In analyzing the task of finding formulas terms" in a number series, Gagne drew a hierarchical diagram of the subordinate skills, arranged in layers, and indicated the sequence in which the subordinate parts of the task should be taught. He theorized that the competencies so higher ones and that starting with the learning of the lowest levels, attaining each higher level depends on positive transfer, recall, and the effects of instruction in guiding thinkings. At the very bottom of the hierarchy may be found relevant competencies supposedly learned earlier and basic abilities relevant to the learning of the task. Gagne administered test items over each competency to ninth-grade boys. Each boy was tested first for the final task; if he failed, the test for the next lowest competency was given and so on down the hierarchy until the boy passed on a competency. At that point the testing stopped temporarily, and learning program designed to teach the next highest competency was administered. Then the test items were given over the remaining levels. The results showed, first of all, that the boys exhibited wide individual differences in patterns on the tests, illustrating different entering competencies. There were no instances in which a person able to perform a higher level competency failed on a lower one. After completing the instructional portion for previously failed competencies, the boy was again tested, yielding scores on competencies both before and after administration of the learning program.

In reference to the abilities at the bottom of such hierarchies, Gagne theorized that if learning program were of perfect effectiveness, everyone would pass all the component tests in the hierarchy, the variance would be zero, and all correlations of tests on the various competencies with basic abilities also would be zero. But if learning program are not perfectly effective, the probability that a person will acquire each competency will be increased to the extent of his score on a test of the basic ability.

Gagne and Paradise dealt with sources of Individual differences in rate of learning from a learning program. They suggested that differences in rate of learning observed among learners are due not to variations on some underlying general ability to learn fast, but rather to (a) the number and kinds of learning sets (competencies, knowledge) the learner brings to the situation, and secondarily; to (b) his standing in respect to certain basic abilities relevant to the competencies to be acquired as they are identified in the theoretical hierarchy for the task and (c) his level of general intelligence. Reasons for failure to learn to perform a task after taking a learning program could be as follows: (a) come subordinate knowledge may have been left out of the learning program; (b) insufficient practice or some other program characteristic may have resulted in poor recall of a subordinate competency; or (c) the program may have been defective in guiding thinking required to induce the necessary integration of subordinate competencies.

Gagne and Paradise hypothesized that a substantial amount of the variability during learning is attributable to the attainment or nonattainment of learning sets relevant to the final task the program is designed to teach "Accordingly, as the learner progresses upwards in the hierarchy, his rate of learning should depend increasingly upon relevant abilities." In contrast, the correlation of general ability with rate of learning should remain constant as the learning progresses up the hierarchy. As contrasted to rate of achievement, the fact of achievement rather than nonachievement in a moderately ineffective learning program might depend increasingly on relevant abilities as one does up the hierarchy, e.g, those of low ability "drop out" due to failure on some competencies while those more ability continue to master competencies in spite of defects in the program. The task of solving linear algebraic equations was selected to test some of the above 'hypotheses. A learning hierarchy was designed by a logical analysis procedure. The resulting hierarchy showed six levels of relevant competencies and at the bottom, three specific relevant abilities.

The Procedure employed in the study by Gagne Paradise was as follows: First, basic ability tests were administered. Then the learning program was given, using eight booklets over eight class days. Then a performance test of solving equations was given, followed at once a transfer test involving unfamiliar forms and unfamiliar Symbols. On the next day, tests were given on each learning set in the hierarchy. Learning rate was recorded by having students draw a line on their program answer sheet on a signal given every three minutes. As to overall achievement on the performance test and transfer tests, the results indicated that the program was only moderately effective.

As to transfer from earning of subordinate sets to higher ones in the hierarchy, students were scored as "pass" or "fail" on test items over each of the component capabilities. Patterns of pass-fail from lower skills to higher ones were then analyzed for each learner. The results for pairs of items for adjacent levels in the hierarchy confirmed theoretical predictions or transfer from one competency to the next in proportions of instances ranging from 0.91 to 1.00.

On the relations between relevant abilities and learning sets, the results generally confirmed the prediction that rate of learning depends decreasingly on relevant abilities, whereas the achievement of the learning set depends increasingly on such abilities as one goes up the hierarchy. There was also evidence for the corollary assumption that since rate of learning comes to depend less on relevant basic abilities, as learning progresses up the hierarchy it does increasingly depend on achievement of successive subordinate competencies.

An implication of the findings is that as learning progresses, relevant abilities will correlate increasingly with achievement only for programs which are somewhat defective in mediating transfer from one level to the next. Further data supporting the general theory of learning hierarchies and the implications for the sequencing of instructions were contained in reports by Gagne and others and Gagne and Bassler.

Individual differences in rate of learning

Because of the factors identified above in determining rate of learning, it should be apparent that just pushing the learner through the program faster is not always a good way to improve learning. On the other hand, self-pacing by the learner is also no universal cure for slow learning. Gropper and Kress presented data to suggest that self-pacing can be nonadaptive to the needs of the learner. Some learners need to be speeded up and some need to be Wowed down to improve the effectiveness and efficiency of learning, If a learner-determined rate is too fast, more errors occur, primarily because of low IQ. Many high IQ learners proceed slowly and inefficiently, while many low IQ learners go fast and ineffectively. But if the pace of presentation is increased for the total group, the error rate increases, and the achievement gap between the low IQ and the high IQ learners increases. It would appear, then, that experimental study of the individual learner's pace and learning record would be one way to proceed to adjust rate appropriately for each, while analysis of errors would be a way to improve mastery of needed subordinate competencies.

Suppes has reported that hi computer-assisted

instruction individual differences in rate are even larger than previously thought. He, cited individual differences in learning rates for drill material paced in rate by the computer. For Russian-English word pairs Suppes found that the optimum size of unit for practice was typically the largest of several units employed. Thus when lists of Russian-English words were presented in different sizes of units as an application of the whole-part question, college students and junior high school students did better practicing a list of 108 items than a list of 6 when time for mastery of the total list was the criterion The results, of course, might not be the same if English-Russian word pairs were employed. His general rule was that when learning is faster than forgetting the experimenter should show all 108 pairs on the first trial. But when forgetting is faster than learning, only one item should be presented; all exposure of a given pair should then be continuous. The mathematics for in between learning rates was given.

It would appear, then, that in the future branching in rate of presentation should become a new variable in research. Many media now employed for group instruction would need eventually to he adapted and employed for individually paced instruction. This may bring more improvement in use of film, for example, than working to improve the photography. Film material should be packed more widely in smaller segments, with responding required, to capitalize fully on the stimulus advantages of this medium.

Branching as a means of individualizing instruction

Crowder introduced a variation of programed instruction first identified as a "scrambled book' and later as intrinsic programing when machines replaced the books. The scrambled book, unlike other books, is not read in page sequence. The learner is given a paragraph or two of information followed by a multiple-choice question. If the learner chooses the correct alternative, he is directed to a page on which he is reminded of why he is right and then directed to another page having new material and another test question. If the learner chooses the wrong answer, he is directed to a page which tells him that he is wrong, with an explanation of why he is wrong, or he is given a hint and directed back to try again. Crowder has also developed electromechanical for presenting intrinsic programs.

These do the "page turning" for the learner, who needs only to push the coded buttons to be told what to do next. One such device was able to present short motion-picture sequences in addition to projecting pages to print. Later it was found by others that branching program lend themselves to computerization.

Branching programs strike most people as eminently sensible. One could reasonably expect that branching programs should be superior to linear program because they appear to provide the information the learner needs when he needs it without his being bothered by superfluous information. It is difficult, therefore, to understand why there is not more evidence showing branching to be superior to linear programs. Results from early experiments have not been especially encouraging. It may be that some of the early comparisons reflected the effects, of inadequate techniques employed in making the decisions to branch ahead or to backtrack.

In recent years, equipment for the student station for computer-assisted instruction has been greatly improved. Early stations were limited to typewriter input. With the use of the cathode ray tube and light gun providing both printed and pictorial display and with the use of filmstrips, movies, and tape recorders in conjunction with the station, a greater range of instructional stimuli can be employed. Also, if accumulated historical data and series of responses made earlier in the program relevant to the next branching decision to be made can become the replacements for branching on the basis of a single test item, future results for branching programs might greatly surpass those for linear programs. Even so, it may be easier to achieve greater gains with computers for drill than for abstract, conceptual material.

Early results, would appear to suggest the need for basing branching on something other than the results of a single test item because of the (a) unreliability of a single item, (b) danger of failing to assess a competency in a relevant way in view of the next steps to be taken, and (c) possible adverse efffects of making errors. At the present time ' then, it is not entirely clear whether the somewhat disappointing results from comparison of linear with branching programs are due to inadequacy in evaluating the student's competence as a basis for branching decisions, to adverse effects of making errors, to removal of needed redundancy from branching programs, to inadequate basic programing, or to upsetting certain sequencing effects which need to remain unchanged, as in the basic linear program.

In general, improved equipment and techniques are needed in order to devise a multimedia capability which combines the response characteristics of programmed instruction, the branching features of computers, and the stimulus advantages employed in film.

There is no standard definition of "size of step." In programmed instruction it has referred variously to (a) how difficult a response is to make, (b) how large a reading segment is presented before a response is required, (c) how much progress toward the goal is represented by one frame, (d) how long it takes the learner too make a response, (e) whether or not the student responds correctly, and (f) how frequently reinforcement occurs.

At any rate, the theory of Skinner that small steps are needed, while adopted widely be linear programmers, has by no means gone unchallenged. Burner has urged huge leaps, alternating on occasion with small steps. Scandura has questioned the relevance of learning theory as a basis for a theory of instruction and has chosen the principle rather than the S-R bond as the basic unit in meaningful learning. Pressey objected to the fractionization of learning into small steps, preferring the larger, learner-determined, flexible size of step made possible by the technique of adjunct auto-instruction Ausubel advocated the use of "advance organizers," introductory statements in the most general, abstract form, to serve as aids to cognitive structuring of subsequent material. Most motion pictures and television programs are apparently developed in the absence of any such concept as size of step.

Nevertheless, under a wide range of conditions, use of some form of explicit (over to covert) responding has been shown to enhance the value of most media of instruction. Providing knowledge of results has had a similar effect, possibly more consistently for multiple-choice adjunct responding than for constructed responses. This latter effect may be in part a function of size of step (difficulty of responding). New techniques are needed to permit the learner to adjust step size to his capabilities without suffering either many errors or tedious, unneeded re-dundancies. Recent evidence suggests that the neglected technique of adjunct autoinstruction needs wider user.

For learners who can read, few confident generalizations can be made as to whether the instructional media should display pictures, sounds, spoken words, or printed words, The review by Travers debunked the widely held notion that simultaneous visual and auditory stimuli, as in motion pictures or television, are consistently superior to one mode of sensory stimulation at a time. A more moot question is the issue of when to employ auditory and when to employ visual stimuli.

Cooper and Gaeth noted that historically the data regarding efficacy of auditory and visual materials have pointed to an interaction of modality with other factors, notably intelligence, reading ability, age, and difficulty of the material. These investigators employed five age-grade levels of learners, two tasks of different degrees of meaningfulness, and two presentation modes. All three main effects-grade, meaningfulness, and modality—were significant. Performance for nouns was best with visual presentation in the fourth grade, while the auditory presentation was best at the twelfth grade. For the nonsense syllables, the visual presentation was consistently better than the auditory. The reported superiority of visual presentation for nouns in grades 4, 5, and 6 and inferiority in grades 10 and 12 is directly contrary to earlier findings by Day and Beach, as reported by Cooper and Gaeth. The investigators noted that while, in general, auditory stimuli are best for easy material and visual for difficult, the best presentation for new and difficult material is a function of the habit system of the learner as developed by personal experience. They concluded that at some point in language development of the person there ceases to lie a functional distinction between the effectiveness of the two modalities, i.e., a welll-educated adult may learn equally well by hearing, or reading.

Rohwer and others presented 24 pairs of objects in the form of pictures of the objects or printed names of the objects to 96 third and sixth-grade children. As each pair was presented, the experimenter spoke aloud one of four kinds of verbalization: (a) the names of the objects, (b) the names of the objects, connected by a conjunction, (c) the names connected by a preposition, or (d) the names connected by a verb. For both older and younger subjects, pictorial materials produced more efficient learning than did the printed names, and verb connectors facilitated acquisition most, followed by prepositions, then conjunctions.

Snow, Tiffin, and Seibert reported that, while finding no main-effect difference in effectiveness between a training film and a live (lecture) presentation, among Ss with low prior knowledge those with an unfavourable attitude toward films learned better by live instruction. In terms of immediate recall, Ss characterized as active., self-assertive, self-assured, and independent learned better by live presentation Those Ss characterized as passive, followers, dependent, and lacking in self-confidence learned slightly more by the film. In a classroom situation, Westley and Saverin reported that Ss seated farthest from the W screen learned best. Fargo and others reported mean scores on a picture vocabulary test to be no different by group TV administration than by the more time-consuming individual administration by an examiner.

James asked 503 basic airmen to express preferences for taking a lesson by reading or by lecture. A no-preference option was permitted. There were no performance differences associated with preference, but for the total sample learning by reading was superior to lecture (.05 level). Preference was unrelated to ability, but the superiority of reading was greater for high-ability airmen. These few experiments lend little evidence arguing for increased use of auditory stimuli for the talks and type of Ss, employed. For high-ability students who are good readers, the reading mode is generally effective. For difficult material, reading permits a backtracking to check uncertain points in a more convenient fashion than backward scanning of a tape recorder. And often a lecturer cannot repeat on request an utterance of an earlier, inspired moment. It is suggested that audio is best for story-like material, for young children, and for poor readers. The new technique of speeded speech and very economical in time for easy material.

As predicted by Schramm, there is some recent indication that research in programed instruction is merging with the mainstream of educational research. In the earlier period, analytical studies in programed instruction tended to center on 'treatments" studies of the esoteric "programing variables" such as size of step, mode of response, item sequence, and the like. Recently personality, intellectual, and cultural variables in the learner are coming to be studied in relation to programed instruction, and "systems" approaches and multimedia instruction have brought more examination of programed instruction as a "component" of instruction. Also the value of empirical methods of developing instructional materials, emphasized heavily by programmers, is coming to be though of by many as the greatest permanent effect of the programed instruction movement.

One study relating a personality variable to a programing was conducted by Campeau. Using a program on earth-sun relationships, she found that among fifth grade girls, those scoring high on text anxiety did best with a program which provided feedback, while those low in anxiety did best with a program without feedback. No significant interaction was found for boys between these two variables.

Lublin reported that college students in introductory psychology scoring high on autonomy need achieved better than those with low need on programed instruction. Autonomy need was determined by score on the Edwards Personal Preference Schedule (EPPS) and was interpreted in terms of liking to work alone without interaction with a teacher. She also reported that for programs with no reinforcement or with variable ratio reinforcement, higher achievement resulted than for programs with continuous reinforcement.

Kight and Sassenrath reported that high-achievement motivated students performed better on three criteria than did students with low-achievement motivation. The criteria were time to complete the program, number of errors, and short-term retention score. High test-anxiety Ss worked faster and made fewer errors than low-anxiety students; but failed to exhibit higher retention scores. This finding of lack of relationship between anxiety level and achievement is not in conflict with the findings by Campeau above, since Campeau's distinction was between programs with and without feedback, and significant results were obtained only for girls.

Doty and Doty reported that achievement through programed instruction appeared to be related to personality characteristics. They reported a nonsignificant correlation between achievement and learning from the program. Also, they reported a high positive correlation between grade point average and attitude towards programed instruction, but no significant correlation between achievement and attitude.

Fiks reported that attitude towards straight reading versus overt-response programs was dependent on the education of Ss and residence in cities or rural areas, although there were no treatment main effects relating to confirmation, response mode, or reading. For persons of low educational levels attitude toward programs was more favorable if confirmation was provided. The reverse was the case for highly educated Ss With covert responding, urban Ss liked program less well than did rural Ss, but with written (overt) responses, urbanites liked programs more than rural Ss. Credence in the programs was reported as more closely related to achievement than was attitude.

Woodruff, Faltz, and Wagner correlated subscores on two personality tests (EPPS) and Gordon Personal with correct responses on program frames. Significant values were 0.53 for achievement motivation, 0.50 for cautiousness, 0.74 for original thinking, 0.81 for persona., relations, and 0.81 for vigor. The correlation of IQ with frames correct was 0.75. Turning from personality and attitudinal variables to intellectual variables in the learner, Buckland administered program of three different response modes (writte., thinking, reading) to Ss of high and low ability. Parallel tests were given immediately after learning and after 27 days. There were no significant differences among response mode treatments at either ability level on either test. But when retention was expressed as gains, there was a significant interaction; high-ability Ss employing written responses were superior to those employing reading, with covert responding falling in between; it was also found that low-ability Ss lost ground over the 27day interval on all modes that of reading.

Williams, employing program as review, compared results or Ss of high and low aptitude. Difference in achievement for these two aptitude groups was, in descending order, constructed response, multiple-choice, emphasis, then reading. Variability in achievement was least for constructed response. She concluded that aptitude makes the greatest difference in achievement for the, less active modes of responding.

Woodruff, Faltz, and Wagner reported significant

correlations for ninth-graders between ability measures and number of frames correct on a program in electricity. For fourth- and fifth-graders, they reported similar high relationships between scores on a reading, test and number of correct responses on a program in spelling

Feldman assigned 144 Ss of high and low verbal ability to one of three programs differing in difficulty level or to corresponding texts of reading material created from the programs by printing in the blank terms so that program and texts would consist of identical words. Two criteria were employed: a pre- and a post-test similar to items in the program and a transfer test of items dissimilar to program items. Verbal ability, diffliculty level, and format were found to be unrelated to gain on the cloze test. But on the transfer test, Ss of high ability did better than those of low ability, Ss of low ability did better from study by text than study by program (.05), and no differences were attributed to difficulty level. There was an interaction of ability with difficulty, suggesting that "'challenging" materials were most effective. The investigator concluded that responding to programs interferes with organization of the material and that well prepared charts in a text can help overcome difficult wording.

Hershberger employed typographical cueing to distinguish core from enrichment materials in written texts and "adjunct self-evaluation test questions interspersed among pages of reading material. Different groups received different combinations of conditions: terse or discursive text, simple or complex typographical cueing, and texts without questions as well as texts with questions. High-ability Ss benefited from either terseness or self-evaluation test items or from both used together. Low-ability Ss, benefited from terseness only if it was accompanied by self-evaluation test items. The test items were a mixture of multiple-choice and constructed response items. For the sample as a whole, self-evaluation questions enhanced learning and retention of core content without detracting from enrichment content. Simple typographical cueing was more effective than complex cueing. The effects of simple cueing and self-test items were independent and additive.

The above experiment on "adjunct autoinstruction" is reported in this section dealing with programed instruction since reviewers consider the adjunct method (using test items with prose material and immediate feedback) as a type of programed instruction. Pressey, however, considers the two methods to be independent and distinct. The only direct comparisons of overall effectiveness of the two methods were reported by Pressey and by Pressey and Kinzer, both finding adjunct at least as effective and much more efficient, especially for terse texts. Hershberger inserted questions after each few pages of reading, depending on the terseness of the text. Frase found effective learning for certain materials and subject by placing multiple-choice test questions after each 120 lines of reading.

Katz reported data suggesting that when different segments of material differ iii difficulty for a task requiring formation of discrimination learning sets, high IQ SS gradually improve regardless of whether successive practice sessions are arranged in order of increasing, decreasing, or unchanging difficulty. For low IQ Ss, however, performance is best with a consistency of problem type and problem difficulty. And after a six-month interval the high IQ Ss benefit more from additional practice than do the low IQ Ss. Considerable research interest recently has been exhibited, especially in England, in comparing the effects of programed instruction as used by an individual for solitary study with effects from smallgroup utilization of programs. Early research comparing "paired" and 'individual* learning from programs used linear programs. In two studies cited by Noble, pairs did better than individuals. Noble also cited a study using intrinsic programs in which individuals performed better than groups of three. Noble further indicated that teachers in England ask about group use of an expensive device for displaying intrinsic program as a possible economy move. Noble arranged eight weeks of learning by three groups of "fourth-form students in a mixed secondary modern school." The three groups were matched oil four variables: age, sex, verbal and mathematics scores, and prior knowledge of trigonometry. Mean age was 153 years. Control groups had one child at a machine; experimental groups had two children working at each machine. Students chose their own work mates. Results less learning by the pairs, although cost economy was achieved. There was no significant attitude difference, but there was a trend in favor of working alone.

Crutchfield and Covington considered creativity as a learner variable in relation to use of programed instruction. They approached the linking of creativity and programs as an apparent paradox to be resolved, since features of programs appear to be antithetical to the requirements for creativity, and offered suggestions for the improvement of programs to enhance creativity. These suggestions included (a) keep the self-packing, self-administering feature; (b) give choice of materials and paths; (c) use diagnostic and evaluative measures to change path when needed; (d) use more flexible kinds of feedback; (e) generate uncommon ideas; (f) lead students to evaluate their own ideas; (g) reward deviant responses; (h) produce reasonable amounts of study work before it is criticized; (i) use actual problems to be solved in their entirety, 0) diversify content on a given topic; and (k) use large steps to create productive tension.

There is current interest among some educators and researchers in discovery of the unique patterns which may distinguish one student's style of learning from another's The topic of personal cognitive style was not reviewed here because of time limitations. The reviewer hazards the conjecture, based or, data such as the series of studies by Gagne and his associates cited earlier, that if one were to design media to adapt media programs rigorously to the individual learner's general ability, special aptitudes, and entering competencies, most of the variance would be accounted for, as compared to such variance as may reflect those characteristics meant by cognitive style. This review generally has not covered comparative effectiveness studies, in which the merits of one medium are compared with another or with 'conventional" instruction on the basis of criterion scores for some selected experimental lesson Criticisms and recommendations for improving this type of study have been covered in previous reviews. The review has been based on the assumption that just as one medium cannot be shown best across the board or even for one subject matter area, so also one can not show that one medium is best for one type of student. Rather, a search was made for studies a which the achievement of learners with particular characteristics was compared with learners having other characteristics when particular media were programed in well defined ways. Said differently, one does not hope to find evidence for matching a medium with a person or subject matter area; instead one seeks to consider learner characteristics while analyzing tasks with respect to the optimum kind of stimuli and learning conditions which can be provided by various media.

Learner variables examined include general and special ability past specific achievement, Personality variables, and demographic characteristics. Results for learners classified by these variables were related to media or programing characteristics including packing, branching, size of step, and modality of stimulation. Results were not particularly clear-cut or consistent among similar studies. For example, one can find instances where students of low verbal ability learned better by reading than by constructed response program and other instances where the reverse was reported. Such differences can arise because of use of a variety of learning task, variations in how skillfully the programing is done, or differences among subjects in amount of relevant prior learning.

Nevertheless, the advent of programed instruction has provided a stimulus and a vehicle for study of such person interactions with program style. A next step would be to take some "Programing variable," such as size of step, defined in any one of several possible ways, and implement variations in size of step for several media for experimental lessons representing several kinds of learning. To date, such variables as size of step are studied mainly with programed instruction, while variables such as simplicity versus embellishment are studied by films. It would be desirable to attempt experimentally to introduce the same variable, in several media and then to introduce matches with learner variables. There is thus some argument for complex interaction studies to assess interaction of person variable by media by programing feature by type of learning.

On the other hand, experiments which compare achievement, under defined instructional conditions, for subgroups of learners identified as high or low IQ do fail to account for other learner variables which may be operating. Thus intensive study of selected individuals learning from a wide variety of media for many kinds of learning objectives would be advisable. One problem in applying the results of such research might be difficulty in incorporating all of the kinds of differences found into manageable media packages. In short, one may find unique sources *of* variance by intensive study *of* individuals, but one may not be able to vary media programs for each unique characteristic.

Some of the variables which have been studied with programed instruction, particularly the effort to sequence instruction in accordance with explicit analyses of the learning objectives into subordinate components, as in the research by Gagne, need to be extended into work with other media. In general the procedure of task analysis, empirical tryout by sequencing studies of validate or correct the task nalysis, followed by further empirical revision, is a good interim model to follow until we have more refined theories of task taxonomies, learner variables, and media variables.

3

Simple Media

Within the realm of educational technology, graphic production refers to the creation of visual educational materials. It is an applied art. Typical products include:

(a) An overhead transparency which shows the plot of an algebraic equation.

(b) A poster which illustrates actions to be taken in the event of a fire.

(c) Art for a slide presentation on the development of the human embryo.

(d) An illustrated pamphlet describing how to conserve energy in the home.

While these products vary considerably in form, the basic processes by Which they are produced are quite similar.

Design

The first step in the graphic production process is design. Good design creates visual materials which clearly communicate their intended message to the intended audience. Factors such as aesthetics are important, but are secondary considerations when compared to effective communication.

At the beginning of the design process, the graphic artist consults with the client to determine the objective and content for each visual, the audience for whom the visuals are intended, the format in which the final product will appear, and any special circumstances affecting the production or use of the visuals.

Using this information, the artist often produces a rough sketch to show how the visuals will appear in their final form. At this point the artist should consider a number of visual design principles.

(a) Clarity—when producing education materials, the most significant principle of visual design is clarity. The purpose of the visual must be obvious to the intended audience. Audience characteristics such as reading level and previous experience should be considered.

(b) Simplicity—one of the most effective ways to insure clarity is through simplicity, Unnecessary or distracting details should be eliminated and, if possible, each visual should be restricted to a single idea.

(c) Emphasis—when visuals are complex, the key elements within the visual should be emphasized to draw the viewer's attention, Methods for emphasis include the use of labels, contrasting colours, or enlarged elements.

(d) Harmony—in order for the key elements to be emphasized, the background elements must not draw attention to themselves. Unless a particular element is to be emphasized, the use of contrasting sizes, type styles, colours, or drawing styles should' be avoided.

(e) Organization the way in which the elements of a visual are organized can have a significant effect on the efficiency with which the information in the visual is perceived. The organization of a visual should be obvious and consistent with cultural practices.

(f) Legibility—textual elements within visuals must be legible, Simple type styles which are large enough to be easily read under a variety of conditions are best.

(g) Balance—visual materials with elements arranged in an unnatural or unbalanced manner call distract viewers. The arrangement of visual elements should appear in balance.

(It) Unity—the separate elements of a visual should create the final effect or one meaningful unit. The unity of a visual can be increased by moving the elements closer together. Other techniques include the use of overlap, borders, or a common background.

Early in the design process, the graphic artist should determine the format for the final product. This information is critical if the produced visuals are to conform comfortably to the characteristics of., the medium. For projected media, the most significant of these characteristics is the aspect ratio, which is the ratio of the height to the width of the projected image. The aspect ratios of common projected media. The size of the art may vary as long as the aspect ratio is maintained,

Illustration

The illustration step involves the creation or manipulation of pictures to be included in the final product. Common sources for pictures include original or reproduced photographs, as well as original, reproduced, or manipulated art.

The form of' an illustration call have a significant impact upon the case and cost of production. For example, a colour photograph is usually more expensive to reproduce than a simple black and white drawing, In this case, the two factors affecting production costs are the use of continuous tone art and the use of multiple colours. When cost is a major consideration, illustrations should be limited to line drawings and to one or two colours. Photography provides one of the most common sources of art for graphic production. Usable photographs may be available from existing resources within the organization or may be acquired from external photographic archives. However, original photographs usually have to be taken or commissioned by the artist or client. Before pictures are taken, the artist should determine if the final product is to be in colour or black and white, and whether a transparency or print is best. Colour transparencies are commonly used in the production of slides, films, or filmstrips, whereas black and white prints are most common for print materials. Most photographic originals are continuous tone and may need to be converted to line art. This is most commonly done by using a dot screen to convert the photograph to a dot pattern, but can also be accomplished using other specialized photographic techniques.

Existing art provides tit abundant source of illustrations. Since the creation of original art can be time consuming, it is common practice to reuse illustrations from other sources such as books, periodicals, and handouts. However, care should be taken to ensure the resulting product conforms to copyright regulations. Often such drawings can be reproduced photographically or on a copy machine and then used intact or modified to meet the needs of a parricular visual.

Clip art services provide copyright-free, ready-made illustrations. Usually such services provide sheets or booklets of' general topic line drawings which have a common theme such as sports, media, or educational scenes. The purchase price of these materials include reproduction rights. Often, however, it is difficult to find an existing illustration which meets the exact requirements of a planned visual. In such cases it becomes necessary to manipulate existing art. Common manipulation techniques include clipping illustrations from a variety of sources and assembling them in a single visual, tracing a continuous tone illustration to convert it to a line drawing, or tracing a key element from one illustration and drawing the other elements of the visual freehand. An extensive, well-organized picture file will greatly facilitate this process.

Original art is often the only option for the artist. For additional information on specific art techniques refer to Kemp or Minor and Frye.

While almost any art medium can be copied, some illustrations are easier to reproduce than others. Where cost or production techniques limit flexibility, continuous tone art should be avoided in favour, of line drawings. Thus pen and ink drawings will usually be much more appropriate than pastel or shaded pencil drawings.

A variety of drawing instruments and aids are available to assist in the illustration process. A visit to the nearest art supply store should provide insight into the range of possibilities.

Lettering

Type is an important component of most educational materials. The type may be as simple as a label or caption, or as extensive as the printed text of a pamphlet. For the purpose or this article, type will be considered in two categories—text type and display type, Text type is relatively small, usually appears in columns, and accounts for the bulk of most printed materials. Display type is larger and is used for headings, labels, application in which the type is designed to attract attention. Many typesetting systems are designed to set either text or display type, not both. Thus many graphic production facilities will require more than one typesetting system.

Photo typesetting refers to a process in which the type font is a photographic negative. Light is used to print an image or the type characters on photographic paper which must he chemically developed before the type becomes visible. These typesetting systems range from the cumbersome and inexpensive to the efficient and ultra-expensive. The more sophisticated versions incorporate a standard typewriter keyboard and a microcomputer system so that the text can be entered and edited prior to being printed. Systems can be purchased which handle text type, display type, or both.

A variety of strike-on lettering devices exist which use the pressure of a raised character against an inked ribbon to create the type image. These devices range from common typewriters to more,, sophisticated versions which offer a variety of type sizes and styles, as well as a range of other options. While most are intended to set text type, the quality of some systems permits the type to be photographically enlarged and used for display purposes. In addition, several relatively inexpensive strike-on systems are now available which use large plastic, disc-shaped fonts to set display type on transparent adhesive tape which can easily be adhered to art. Mechanical lettering systems offer a relatively inexpensive method or producing quality type, Most systems either use a stencil through which a tracing pen is inserted, or a grooved template in which the point of a mechanical scriber traces out the shape of the letter. Such systems are designed primarily for creating display type and require some skill on the part of the artist.

Dry transfer type is a system by which the artist uses a burnishing tool to transfer letters to the finished art from large translucent sheets. The material is available in a wide variety of sizes and styles, but is intended primarily for display purposes, While the process is relatively inexpensive for small quantities of type, application is tedious and alignment can be difficult. Artists with limited resources or exceptional talent should consider hand lettering as an option. Carefully executed hand lettering can equal or surpass the lettering quality of some of the mechanical systems. The use of guidelines and a consistent style is recommended. A variety of style manuals are available to aid artists in the development of their hand lettering technique.

Assembly

Assembly is the positioning of visual elements for reproduction. When preparing materials to be printed, the resulting product is frequently called a paste-up or a mechanical. However, the same step can also result in the assembly of slide flats, filmstrip flats, mounted pictures, or displays. A variety of adhesives are available for use during the assembly process and selection or a specific adhesive depend upon the intended use of the product. Under varying circumstances the artist may use an adhesive that is permanent, removable, or temporarily repositionable.

Rubber cement is one of the most common and flexible adhesives available anti call result in either a permanent or removable bond. In addition, several manufacturers provide a special "one-coat" version which remains tacky and repositionable for months after application.

Units which do a lot of paste-up work often use waxers which apply narrow strips of melted wax to the back of the art. Wax bonds are repositionable, but adhere reasonably well when burnished properly.

Dry mounting provides another common tool for the assembly process. In this case a sheet of heat-sensitive material is placed between the two surfaces to be adhered arid it dry mount press is used to apply heat arid pressure. The system also provides an excellent means of laminating visual materials for protection from moisture or dirt. Other common adhesives include sprays, tapes, and glues.

A major concern of the assembly process is the proper alignment of the visual elements. A variety of tools assist the graphic artist with this task. The most common of these are the drawing board T-square, triangle, and ruler.

Reproduction

Reproduction is the conversion of visual products from intermediate to final forms. It is the most diverse of the production steps, with each process having its own specific requirements and procedures.

For example, an assembled thermal overhead transparency master must be approximately 8 x 10 and should consist of carbon based images on white paper. It is reproduced by laying a sheet of thermal transparency film on the master and inserting it in a thermal copier,

On the other hand if a diazo transparency is required, the master must have ;in opaque image on a translucent or transparent base, the transparency is made by exposing the master to ultraviolet light in contact with diazo film, the film is then developed in ammonia fumes.

If the desired product is a 35mm slide, the art may be in colour arid of any reasonable size, but it must conform to the 2:3 aspect ratio. In this case, reproduction requires a 35mm camera, a copystand, arid appropriate lighting.

Other reproduction processes will have requirements and procedures which are its diverse as the examples given, Readers are also referred to Kemp as well as Minor arid Frye.

Graphic production facilities

Graphic production facilities vary, depending upon the size of the staff and the types of products which are produced. However, certain feature are typically found in all units. Basic drawing tools, a good working surface, and one or more lettering systems are essential. Also needed are storage space for supplies, a papercutter, it sink, and ;in assortment of specialized reproduction devices.

4

Educational Telecasting

Investigation of the national picture for television for school and community brings to light the fact that most valuable use of educational television is being made in schools and colleges which are using their firs, appropriations for closed-circuit facilities. Many institutions are becoming acquainted with TV techniques in this way prior to starting non-commercial stations. This arrangement is comparable to a central sound System. "Wired" television it is, which brings programs to all the rooms of the building that are equipped with TV receivers. Performances are put on as if they were regular live telecasts. Although they are not sent out on the air, they may be preserved by adding to the closed-circuit equipment a kinescope recorder and a processor. In this way the programs become 16-mm. films.

The equipment purchased for the closed-circuit studio may be used later in a station, for it comprises such basic essentials as a two-camera chain, lighting, and audio and video equipment. When the budget permits, kinescope-recording equipment and processor may be added, and you are ready to enter the exchange of programs market, bringing publicity to your institution through circulating your programs among institutions, schools, and television stations. Kinescope may be shown on regular 16-mm projectors in or outside a studio, and programs thus become available to schools and Community organizations not yet equipped for television. The closed-circuit plan is an ideal one for teacher training institutions, as Kansas State College, Manhattan, as proved, or for the teaching of medicine, as used by the University of Kansas, where color has been added to the closed-circuit scheme. Stephens College, Missouri, was one of the earliest users of the closed-circuit campus arrangement. The University of North Carolina began its television activities with the closed circuit, renting kinescoping equipment to preserve initial programs.

The state of Wisconsin chose to start its TV activity, designed to utilize twelve channels eventually, with a closed-circuit "station" at the university in Madison. As a laboratory for teaching and research, it contains three camera chains, cable to link studio and the viewing the rooms, lighting and scenery, monitors, a mobile unit, photographic equipment, a kinescope recorder, and a processor. Here is an adequate beginning with essential equipment, for training, students, developing television courses on undergraduate and graduate levels, and giving the staff an opportunity to experiment in programming and production techniques before actually being faced with a complicated broadcasting-station schedule.

Even without a budget some of our institutions are managing to go into full-scale television training. Schools and colleges in locations were commercial broadcasters are waiting for the FCC go-ahead and have a purchased all their studio equipment, my find it possible to develop Closed-circuit telecasts along the plan used by Denver University. Recipient of a loan of over $50,000 worth of equipment from station KNZ. Denver, this university produced experimental shows and developed excellent workshop courses. A full-time university instructor supervised tine workshop, with the technical side in the hands of three engineers loaned by Station KLZ. A TV research specialist from the station evaluated the experiment.

The variable closed-circuit studio is also used for rehearsing on the campus or in the school building prior to taking the "packaged" show to the local station for telecasting. The Creighton University, Omaha, television staff ha, even gone so far in this stimulated campus setup as to design, a 'rehearsal camera " complete with action lights, corresponding in shape and size to an electronic television camera. It has a dummy lens turret in front and pilot lights in various positions to familiarize the cast with the presence of cameras and to instruct them on facing the camera in operation. It is mounted on a tripod and dolly, has view-finding lenses which respond to variations in position, and is equipped with a cable input for bringing in the electric power line from the switching unit as well as the audio lines.

In anticipation of participating in the programming of Chicago's non-commercial station, the South Shore High School uses a "homemade" TV studio developed by Philip Lewis. His plan may be applied to any elementary; school or college without a TV budget.

Education is accustomed to operating on a shoestring. There are ways and most interesting means non commercial TV stations to save money. Since selling education is a national endeavour, communities save, as commercial stations cannot, by exchanging programs. Our biggest television network is the world's cheapest yet one of the best—the United States mail.

This exchange is made possible by equipping each educational producing unit, or station, with 'Kinescoping facilities so that each may record its creative programming. This permanent packaging of original telecast on film makes it possible to ship programs to other stations for retelecasting at convenient local hours.

"Imagine," says E. Arthur Hungerford, engineering, consultant for the JCET, "fifty educational stations operating. If each produced locally one 15-minute program per day which was useful to the other fifty educational stations, there would be over twelve hours of programming available each day for every station at one-fiftieth of the cost of doing the original program."

A kinescope is made by photographing the images on a bright television picture tube and recording the sound track at the same time. It is easily shipped by mail and is retelevised exactly as one would handle a 16-mm movie on a station projector or on a standard school projector. The image orthicon studio camera used for live telecasts also transmits these kinescopes. A small motion-picture screen, 11 by 14 inches or smaller, is substituted for the 4- by 3-inch iconoscope plate.

The most powerful way to make educational television an integral part of the culture of our country is to see that program are made available to other communities and institutions. That is why each producing unit should acquire its own kinescoping facilities as early in the basic planning for a station as is financially possible. Until they are able to kinescope or film their programs, producers should have available for exchange scripts or production outlines and join in the exchange of ideas for programming.

The sound may even be put on tape and be found, with a little editing, to carry the original purpose of the show in a radio version. Students may see a kinescope from another school and be most interested in the subject, matter but wish to develop it along their own line of creative thinking. In this way the educational value of the program lives on. While network facilities, even though state-wide, cannot be available to all educational TV groups, this interchange of programs is possible without too great a financial burden on any one institution. One of the primary differences between educational and commercial television is the "fleeting art" characteristic of commercial programs. Once they are telecast a majority of them disappear from air, for they have been already "sold," while educational program are being preserved from the very of non-commercial television.

In our search for ways to further understanding abroad we find that kinescopes make possible an interchange of programs between countries, with the native tongue added to the sound track. Most countries have different standards of television transmission, but methods of film projection are standardized throughout the world. An exchange of educational kinescope between countries opens the quickest avenue for international television. Through the initiative of the National Association of Educational Broadcasters such an exchange is becoming a reality.

Basic station equipment

The broadcasting of visual images by electronics is a highly complicated process, challenging leaders in the electrical and engineering fields to improve and simplify equipment from year to year. Remote-control boxes for TV cameras and stronger amplifying tubes for increasing UHF transmitter power Lire typical of strides forward in perfecting the technical aspects of television. Equipment manufacturers are meeting the challenge of non-commercial television along with educators.

Despite the fact that construction and equipment costs fluctuate, it is important to include here tangible information upon which we may begin our individual figuring. Cost estimates are inevitable points of argument. Commercial calculations are considered unduly high by most educators, who have equipped their studios for less than the estimates made by equipment manufacturers.

Basic station equipment includes a transmitter for picture and sound; a studio with two cameras and sound are lighting equipment; film-projection facilities, and a kinescope recorder as well as a processor for finishing local newsreels and kinescopes.

Like Minnesota and Wisconsin, states not wishing to finance more than one or two television stations may plan to extend their coverage by operating several relay stations made up of a transmitter for picture and sound which relays the programs to extended areas. Connected to the central station by microwave links, it is thus possible to distribute programs throughout the state. A list of essential equipment includes a TV picture transmitter, a sound transmitter, an antenna system to radiate the picture and sound, and the microwave link receiver to deliver the picture and sound from the television station. The relay station is housed in a small building. The overall Post of the antenna and equipment runs around $ 125,000. Maintenance costs of this relay station are a fraction of the operating costs of the central station originating the programs.

JCET consulting engineer E. Arthur Hungerfold itemizes equipment costs for community groups. The following figures are his estimates. He points out that the cost of building an educational station may vary from $ 150,000 to $ 750,000, depending on equipment and size of plant. On the average, annual operating expenditure can be expected to run to at least $ 100,000.

Equipment manufacturers vary somewhat in prices, but $ 250,000 stands as an average capital-investment figure. This does not take into consideration local economies, such as antenna sharing the local stations, studio space in school or community buildings, and film equipment which is already owned by a great many educational institutions.

A major addition to make when finances permit is a mobile unit for on-the-spot telecasting throughout the station area. Cameras for this unit are interchangeable with studio cameras, making it possible to augment facilities in the field or station. A microwave link sends the program from the mobile unit to the studio.

Most institutions of higher learning are managing spread the initial cost of television equipment. For example, the completely equipped television studio of the University of Southern California cost a little over $ 100,000. This included remodelling of part of Hancock Hall for the studio. The university's radio station is in this same building. The studio equipment includes two cameras, a film-chain camera for projection of movies and slides, monitoring sets for the control room, generators, and lights. The university also purchased 1,00,0 feet of extra cable so that cameras may be moved to the scientific-research laboratories in the same building.

Iowa state College has owned its own AM radio station since 1921. In 1949 construction was completed for an FM station with a 580-foot tower suitable for the supporting structure for the TV antenna as well. Fully six months after the FM station was or, the air, the TV construction was completed, and WOI-TV went on the air in February, 1950. By splitting construction phases it was possible to spread the costs over a greater length of time, avoiding a single large appropriation.

Those who are holding back because of costs will] find revealing the inexpensive growth of WOI-TV. Its first studios were situated in a remodelled portion of WOI's radio lobby on the third floor of the Service Building. Later the studios were moved to the Exhibit Hall, half of which is now entirely remodelled to house a

46 by 80-foot studio and adjoining control rooms. On the floor above are news and film offices. Production offices and dressing rooms are off the main lobby. Behind the main control room is headquarters for the continuity department. Engineering maintenance and set-design shops are located at the back of the building.

In one corner of the studio may be found a permanent kitchen, which is an essential part of the homemaking programs from this landgrant institution, busy with programs of a vocational nature for men and women. WOI-TV is now equipped to transmit color.

In 1951, after two years of experimentation with monochrome, the University of Kansas School of' Medicine initiated color in educational TV with a budget-wise plan consisting of a single vericolor camera permanently mounted in an operating room in the fifth-floor surgical unit. The camera is mounted vertically above the operative field with its optical system aligned directly in *the* axis of a Specially designed Wilmot Castle operating light. The two lens turret of the camera is rotated remotely at the control area on the floor above, overlooking the surgery area. Motor generator and power-supply fixtures are housed in an adjacent utility room. A closed-circuit arrangement feeds the Picture to an auditorium in the basement of an adjoining building, where a projection system displays an image 6 by 8 feet. The camera, control unit, and power supply for this early Remington Rand-CBS color system cost approximately 27,000. The remotely controlled tilt-pan unit cost between $3,000 and $41,000, and the Wilmot-Castle operating light cost about $2,500.

Wide experimentation in color by equipment manufacturers since 1951 has opened exciting possibilities in the use of flexible studio-type camera chains costing from $30,000 to $40,000, with a probability of price reduction as the demand for them increases. The estimate includes the camera, a camera control unit, and' the, power supply. Dr. Paul W. Schafer, Chairman of the Department Surgery, discusses the university's plan to use this new type of camera in the gradual expansion of their TV teaching *by* placing these cameras in new hospital units with adjacent studio and program-direction areas and by linking, through microwave transmission, the Kansas City, Kansas, Medical center with nearby private hospitals affiliated with ',he undergraduate teaching program, with the Veterans Administration Hospital 10 miles away, and, by means of two-way linkage, with the non-commercial station on the Lawrence campus 40 miles away. Into the picture also comes the plan for a 70-mile microwave linkage of this station with the educational station at Kansas State College in Manhattan.

The blueprint of the television plant of Michigan State College is an excellent example of the physical setup for an educational station.

The television studio has a number of special requirements. The ceiling needs to be quite high for finer and more flexible acoustical properties. The use of overhead lighting demands the extra space, too, and helps to keep the floor space clear for cameras, settings, cast and crews. Side walls should be equipped with movable absorbing panels to vary reverberation so that different effects may he obtainable in a single studio.

Lighting equipment should be kept as flexible as passible an i always adjustable so that it will not interfere with the positioning of cameras and sets. Illumination of the television studio for varying effects is under constant experimentation. Expert advice, including the viewpoints of professional lighting technicians and cameramen, technical directors, and equipment manufacturers, should guide this phase of purchasing. Wise selection will add to the pleasure of experimental productions and prevent unimaginative "flat" lighting from giving a sameness to programs. Lighting equipment selected for ,he studio must be easily and rapidly controlled: glare must be anticipated and avoided. Undue warmth in the studio from the lights should be prevented as much as possible. Air conditioning sometimes becomes an added but necessary expense.

Station KUHT, the non-commercial station owned by the University of Houston, is equipped with three 2,000-watts spots, eight 1,000-watt and two 500-watt floods for general illumination For back-lighting fifteen 1,000watt spots and fifteen 750-watt spots are used for modelling and accent lights. Nine floor-stand lights fitted with various types of light are used for fill-ins. Mounted on the cameras are 150-watt eye lights. A special-effects light is used for backgrounds, and four 1,200-watt strip light, available for the sky cyclorama and other backings. Art director George Collins designed his own dimmer, composed of twelve 2000-watt dimmers, coupled with 60 output circuits in the switching panel. He uses a light crew of four for the average program.

Storage space in or near the studio is essential for Drops and costumes. There should be space for set building and painting and for dressing and make up rooms. In the studio every possible guard against electrical hazards should be taken Installation of sprinkler systems and fireproofing of walls should he included in studio costs. Knowledge of local fire laws at the planning stage will save costly changes later.

Operating costs and personnel

Operating costs are minimized in educational television by the use of teachers and students and supervisory personnel and present a very different financial-budgeting problem from that of commercial stations. Technical schools use the television equipment for laboratory purposes, giving credit to advanced students working under the close supervision of their instructors, or engineers employed to handle transmitter and studio operations and maintenance workers. When television activity is A total effort of a large university excellent arrangements can be made through the various departments by shifting trained personnel to permanent positions in the television development and drawing on departmental budgets already set up.

The operating staff should include transmitter and maintenance engineers and staff, studio cameramen, audio and video, engineers, projectionist, director and floor assistants, lighting technician and crew, art director, scenery and props crew, mike-boom operator, sound-effects technicians, dolly man, wardrobe crew, make-up crew, writers, and administrative and office personnel. Students-in-training usually comprise the crews and often assume entire productions in colleges and universities.

Equipment manufacturers figure yearly operating costs to run about half the construction cost. Items include power to run the transmitter, based on 100 hours per month, a total of about $5,000. Tube cost averages $3,000, general maintenance about $2,000. Maintenance, audio, and video engineers' salaries run between $5,000 and $ 6,000 each.

The operating personnel for the Michigan State College television plant the extensive staff necessary to sustain this non-commercial station. However, students training in TV techniques cut down operational costs so that they cannot be compared with those of typical commercial stations. A 135-member radio-television staff at WOI-AM-FM-TV, including at least 30 college students, keeps that educational station running eleven hours daily. As Station KUHT, Houston, about 150 student volunteers are used. They sign up for specific work, which may be done under the supervision of chief engineer William Davis and his staff of four engineers or head cameraman Robert Werbel and his assistant Phil Zimmerman, who select at least twelve of the students training in TV production Art director George Collins and his assistant, Gene Milligan, a graduate student, use student crews entirely, even in building the six basic sets made up of twenty flats which form the basic backgrounds for the station's many live programs. Houston stores furnish all the props for each setting. The Houston Chronicle donates daily AP news photo service and a leased new wire. With lively community support and student training of this practical nature, it is possible to keep operating costs of non-commercial stations far below typical operating budgets.

5

Instructional Technology

The newness of change itself are characteristics of our times. According to Finn any concept of instructional technology must, in addition to men, machines, materials, and the like include, organization patterns. Technology is a term which is frequently applied loosely and some times erroneously. It means actually more than scientific development, more than engineering achievement, more than mechanical force or the harnessing of energy. Technology is, in fact, the sum total of all the tools and techniques through which men have added leverage to the human effort since the beginning of time... (it) is a force which brings together invention, skills and techniques, machinery and equipment, men, money and methods "Technology has succeeded spectaularly in America because we have rejected the thesis of man as a beast of burden and valued his ingenuity above his physical strength. The pursuit of a definition of technology and then the application of that definition to evaluation can be carried great distances.

Finn observed, properly constructed, the concept of instructional or educational technology is totally integrative. It provides a common ground for all professionals, no matter in what aspect of the field they are working, it permits the rational development and integration of new devices, materials and methods as they come along. In this way, Finn has recommended the overtaking of the professional responsibilities of educational technology by the educationists.

> ... The most significant factor of the coming technological are may well be the new man-machine partnership in intellectual activities. The next decade will see the advent of the period in which electronic machines become highly active in the intellectual activities of the world, in which the capacity for gathering and using information, the overall brainpower of the world, is increaded by many fold....

The next decade of which Simon Ramo speaks is now but five years away. These years will be, as we grow older five years that will pass an acceleration which is incredible. Already the sites for the 1970 and 1971 national conventions are being considered. And in the meantime, of course, the physicists will have to deal with twice as much information as they have today, the biologists and biochemists may have cracked the riddle of cancer, and the supersonic aircraft will be an approaching reality, if not an actuality.

The speed and, as Robert Oppenheimer once said, the newness of change itself are characteristics of our times. In facing this time of accelerating change in which nothing will remain totally static, the membership of the Department of Audiovisual Instruction has an option It can elect to state its self-image in a name which is static or backward-looking, or it can opt for the future and say to the world in general and the educational community in particular that its members bear the standard of the educational future. That is all the choice there is.

The proposal, pointed only to the future, therefore, is that the membership vote to adopt either one of two names: the Department of Instructional Technology or Department of Educational Technology. One should like now to present the argument in detail for this point of view—under the constraints stated by the chairman of this symposium, Donald Ely. These constraints require that other name proposals not be criticized, but that positive arguments be offered for the point of view of the advocate. These are commendable and virtuous restraints, but they would have made the writing of the Declaration of independence rather difficult. For when something new if offered, it is almost necessary to criticize the old in order to show why the new fits the situation better.

The concept of an educational or instructional technology is not comforting; on the other hand, a thorough examination of the concept will remove a whole series of artificial objections and make way for the adventure of the future.

Consider "technology" itself. Apparently some people object to the word because it means, they say, machines. If these people are audiovisual types, what they do; do they have special bushel baskets in the rear of the room under which they hide the projectors? As I shall show later the exclusive machine definition of technology is completely wrong and the product of literary-oriented scribblers, but let us follow it for a while anyway. If our business has nothing to do with machines, we are the greatest collection of witch doctors this side of the Congo. We can cause images to appear in the air and sounds to emerge from walls by burning the tail hair of a Siberian Mammoth.

Say the anti-machinesters, you are kidding. We know we have machines, but let's keep it quiet, lies the materials that count—you know, films, tapes, slides, that sort of staff. The machines are just there. Now, that is an interesting argument when you think about it. It presupposes that other machines work on nothing, but that our machines are something special in that they work on materials—and it's, the materials that count. Do drill pressees punch holes in air? Do telephones carry silence? Does a tractor plow ozone? Functionally, does a film exist without a projector, a TV program without a tube, or a still picture without a camera? And you can turn it around, you know. The projector is a nothing without the film. As a postscript, the projector isn't much without a good film; on the other hand, the walls of this philosophic trap close in when we can't project a good film because of a burned-out bulb.

The argument is turned on the point that machines and materials together must be part of the system. Ah, say our mythieal opponents, but you are forgetting the most important item of all—people. Without them, your materials and your machines are meaningless—and, since technology, after all, only deals with machines and materials, we must find another name such as communication or instruction or something that says only people count. This argument is a little more complex. It hinges on such ideas as, "It's what you do with that counts." Such a statement might come close to winning a prize for the cliche of the century if it didn't appear in professional educational writing, where it continues to be treated as if it were emblazoned on the shield of Henry IV freshly discovered in some new diggings under Westminister Abbey..

This point is freely admitted. But it so obvious as almost be nonsense. Even the simple technician in the automobile factory does not use his drill press to punch holes in Swiss cheese, and very few farmers plow sea water. Any teacher, trainer or Harvard professor who uses the wrong machines, materials and techniques for an instructional job is a poor workman; he is as much a part of the technology as the machine or the material and should be put to right, one way or another. The point is that any technology includes humans and the human element. That is what is meant by a *man-machine system.* And I challenge any member of this symposium or any member of DAVI to show me that a teacher using a film in a classroom is not a man-machine system in miniature.

There are those who will say that the job of most members of DAVI is, somehow, administrative and that, therefore, technology has little to do with the job description. Organization is, as the French say, technique. What is being organized is also technique. Any concept of instructional technology must, in addition to men, machines, materials, and the like, include organization pattern.

We are now ready for a technical definition of technology. In other discussions of this problem, I have cited Beard and Hoban among others and no one seems to pay a great deal of attention Let me try again—this time with Henry B. duPont, who said:

> Technology is a term which is frequently applied loosely and sometimes erroneously. It means actually more than scientific development, more than engineering achievement, more than mechanical force or the harnessing of energy. Technology is, in fact, the sum total of all the tools and techniques through which men have added leverage to the human effort since the beginning of time.... is a force which brings together invention, skills and techniques, machinery and equipment, men, money and methods. It is motivated by the question, 'How can we accomplish a desired result at the lowest cost in terms of money, time and, above all, of Physical Output to the end that our resources, our time and our energies can be made available for further advances?" Technology has succeeded spectacularly in America because we have rejected the thesis of man as a beast of burden and valued his ingenuity above his physical strength.

The Pursuit of a definition of technology and then

the application of that definition to education can be carried great distances. For example, the French sociologist Ellul takes somewhat over 50 pages on definition and then keeps throwing in additional material throughout the first part of his book. Machines, materials, methods of use, systems are all part of the pattern of rational mechanisms operating as means to educational ends. And, as Hoban has said, machines are central to this concept even if alone they are not technology.. This is my answer to Lumsdaine.

If, as an Organization of professionals, we understand what technology is and understand that our jobs, whatever they may be—Producer, designer, administrator, research worker, teacher, educator—are the management and operation of the technological function within the social institution of education at any level, we have a future, we have a great adventure, we have a job to do. If we do not understand this fundamental, we will be assailed by each new device and process; we will continue to splinter; we will be left behind either managing a warehouse full of materials, stuck in some audiovisual corner watching others pass us by, or chasing the will-o-the-wisp of something called communications.

Properly constructed, the concept of instructional or educational technology is totally integrative. It provides a Common ground for all Professionals, no matter in what aspect of the field they are working; it permits the rational development and integration of new devices, materials and methods as they come alone. The concept is so completely viable that it will not only provide new status for our group, but will, for the first time; threaten the status of others. We can, make no other choice but to call ourselves the Department of Instructional Technology.

In spite of the clichés currently in vogue about the progress and challenges of professionalism in the educational media field today, a hard, honest look at the problem reveals that our business, field, proffession—whatever you choose to call it—is actually in serious trouble.

It is the thesis of this article that traditional concepts about the professionalism of the educational media field will probably have to be changed and that the organization of DAVI ought to be changed in order to accomodate the demand of the times on the media man. For the media man must be, and must always remain, marginal to many fields, organizations, events, and institutions, and any move toward greater professionalism must take this stubborn fact into account.

The statement that we are in trouble can be countered by overwhelming evidence that the educational communications field as a professional specialization is not only not in trouble, but is enjoying its best days. And here is the beginning of what might be called the great professional paradox. On one hand, it is true that the audiovisual communication field has been growing; its practitioners are becoming more professional; and its many professional contributions to American education over the last 30 years finally are being recognized. On the other hand, increasingly it seems, our destiny is being taken out of our hands; we are gradually being demeaned; and the educational media field, once our domain, is now either too important to be left to educational media specialists or too insignificant to admit the importance—or even the existence—of the need for an educational media specialist, except as he temporarily may be useful as a technician in repairing a projector, hooking up a TV set, or, in extreme cases, locating a film that the librarian could not find.

Money, which is equivalent to energy, was inserted into American education during the years following 1952 by the great foundations and the federal government for the development and use of audiovisual communication devices and materials. Title III of the National Defense Education Act, for example, which provided the school systems of America with a great deal of equipment and materials, forced a certain amount of professional direction upon both state departments of education and school districts. Title VII, the research and dissemination title, had been expanding the intellectual horizons of the media field since its first implementation in 1958 or 1959. Other legislative programs associated with the Great Society concept of the Johnson administration are all having these same effects.

In response, professional programs for training and development have shown some increase. At this writing, approximately 20 NDEA fellows are working on doctorates in the educational communications field in four institutions of higher education. There were over 35 institutes for educational media specialists in the summer of 1965, funded under Title XII of the NDEA. Other graduate programs within a small cluster of institutions have shown increases. Placement requests for instructional technologists with the doctorate are impossible to fill at the present time.

Finally, the professional organizations have grown as well DAVI had approximately 1,200 members in 1952. It now enrolls 6,000. The National Association of Educational Broadcasters was recognized and refinanced during this period and has now become very powerful The National Society for Programmed instruction was founded. Both NAEB and NSPI have engaged in joint projects with DAVI. The Educational Media Council was created about 1961 and now includes representatives of 14 national organizations and maintains headquarters in

Washington, D.C. Professional organizations outside of the field, such as the American Association of Colleges for Teacher Education and the Association for Higher Education, have become interested in media.

Space prevents a further catalog of events, organizations and achievements which point to great professional development on the part of the educational communications field. Enough has been said, however, to make the case. And the case sounds great. The only trouble with the case is that it is true only if you look at it from the optimistic side. For the paradox in which we live our professional lives is that while things professional in the audiovisual field seem very good, they are also very, very bad.

Let us now make the case for retrogression of professional development in audiovisual communication. The positive development of the field described above did happen. However, while it was happening, somebody else picked up and carried off most of the balls in the park. We had a few short, stories—from about 1952 to about 1958—to achieve true professional status and, at least, give some effective professional direction to the field. The truth of the matter is that we didn't make it. And this writing it remains in the balance whether we ever will. The case for retrogression may be seen most clearly by examining two factors: the downgrading of the educational media field by the U.S. Office of Education and the complete lack of attention given to educational media at the White House Conference.

The Commissioner of Education, Mr. Francis Keppel, recently reorganized the U.S. Office of Education. In the process, he wiped out the Educational Media Branch, separating the functions of Title VII-A and Title VII-B within the larger bureaucracy. At least for Title VII-B projects, the monitoring of the projects will be scattered throughout the Office; for example, the monitor of the new contract of the Educational Media Council is to be a nonmedia person. Since Dr. Walter Stone left the U.S. Office a few years ago, where he was the head of the Media Branch, the Commissioner has never replaced him. Seth Spaulding, Thomas Clemens, and John Gough all occupied the position on an acting basis. Several other excellent professionals have paraded swiftly through the Media Branch, either back to where they came from or on to better things, notably Gerald Torkelson and Hugh McKeegan. Obviously, if Commissioner Keepel had any concern at all for the media field, he would have obtained and appointed a permanent head long ago and made conditions such that the parade of experts might have stopped short of a general exodus. Now the Commissioner doesn't need to concern himself—the Branch is gone.

The Commissioners recent decision not to allow the proposed revision of the Educational Media Index to continue as the unique partnership it was between the government, private industry, and the Educational Media Council, but rather to force it into the public domain, was a direct blow at the field of instructional technology and a direct measure of the significance the field has within USOE thinking. Finally, the support and conduct of the New Media Demonstration Center within the U.S. Office is almost a scandal. The Center was grandly conceived as a place where school people from the United States and abroad could see all types of new equipment and materials in a demonstration situation. To that end, many manufacturers and producers, with high hopes, I am sure, placed their equipment and materials in the Center. The Center has gradually declined into a sort of unofficial audiovisual service for USOE agencies, and the room is considered an adjunct meeting room for USOE staff functions. In my last two visits there, much of the demonstration equipment was piled into the corners gathering dust. I hasten to add that it was not the fault of the staff asigned to manage the' operation. The staff was too small, overlooked and lacked the proper logistical support to do a good job. It can be concluded that the Commissioner does not even care about the public image the media field has within the U.S. Office of Education.

The much publicized White House Conference on Education held in July of this year erased any doubts as to the group now running American education for any person at all knowledgeable concerning the national educational scene. The New Educational Establishment which has been put together in the last 15 years was revealed in all its glory from Grandfather James Bryant Conant on down the line.

Although there were political, geographical and other dimensions associated with the invitations in addition to educational eligibility, the fact remains that only two members of the old-line audiovisual field were invited as participants—and they were there by virtue of the fact that they had worked on the Educators for Johnson and Humphery National Committee during the last campaign, not for their connections with the educational media field. As far as I know, the only other people associated one way or another with educational communications were a couple of programmed learning specialists from industry, several big-time publishers, and, of course, Senator Benton and his associates from Encyclopaedia Britannica.

The program was also revealing. Many of the panel topics might or might not have had representatives from the media field, as, for example, "Pre-School Education." However, it would be expected that the two panels on educational innovation—one for elementary and secondary schools and one for higher institutions ought to have had such representation since much of what is referred to as educational innovation either is or is related to educational technology. The closest one might come to this requirement was the fact that Alvin C. Eurich, formerly of the Fund for the Advancement of Education of the Ford Foundation, was on the panel for innovations in higher education. While Dr. Eurich has had more influence on the audiovisual field than most of us put together, it is stretching a point to consider him as a professional representative.

Further, the vice-chairman of the Conference in charge of these two panels—Dr. Ralph Tyler, director of the Center for Advanced Study in the Behavioral Science—could hardly plead ignorance. After all, his brother Keith has had his entire professional career in the educational broadcasting field. The conclusion is inescapable: From the point of view of the planners and directors of the White House Conference, the educational media field deserved no attention whatever.

One of the major addresses of the Conference was given by Dr. Tyler under the title, "Innovations in Our Schools and Colleges". In this address he did mention educational technology as one of five promising areas of innovation. It could be argued, there, that there was some consideration. However, from the professional point of view of people who have pledged their careers to educational media, his words are hardly comforting. Read this quotation carefully:

At the present time, however, the yield from the innovative efforts has been small. Too many of the projects undertaken have been guided by those whose training and competence are in the technology and they have not been wholly familiar with the educational tasks, the aims sought, the conditions of learning to be maintained, and the like. However, today some experiments have been started by persons who have the educational competence as well as having knowledge of the technology being used. We need many more efforts of this sort.....

Dr. Tyler is plainly saying that, in his opinion, the audiovisual or educational media isn't good enough and that other educators must take over his function. There were also two consultants' papers which had bearing on the media field. These papers paralleled the two sections on innovation. One, by Professor Lewis B. Mayhew of the Stanford School of Education, was concerned with innovation in higher education and devoted a great deal of space to the newer educational media. Professor Mayhew quoted extensively from the Stephens College report of 1959, a well-known document in our field. He also referred to some newer developments, such as Florida Atlantic University. Significantly, there is no evidence that Professor Mayhew was acquainted with the DAVI-AHE book on newer media in higher education. That, and his reliance on a 1959 statement in 1965 during a period of accelerating change, suggests that his acquaintance with our field and with the central literature is woefully inadequate. Of course, a scholar would not go looking for literature generated within a profession that he didn't know existed... and that is hardly his fault.

Professor Dwight W. Allen, also of Stanford, prepared the paper on innovations in elementary and secondary education He devoted about two paragraphs to media, but since he was considering innovation broadly, this seems fair enough. In general, he took the Trump position with respect to audiovisual communication devices and materials. Nothing in either of these papers suggests the need for professional direction of media programs, the existence of a professional media literature, or even of media professionals. The conclusion one is forced to come to is that, in the eyes of the Establishment, such media programs, after all are pretty simple and can be managed by any amateur. Finally, the discussion in the two meetings on innovation merely reinforced the general trend of downgrading instructional technology. In effect, all of the discussion could be summarized as stating somewhere fairly early in the proceedings that there were such ' things as films, television and teaching machines; that such things had their small place; and that it was now time to get on with the business of talking about innovation. The cavalier shunting of the audiovisual field to one side early in the meetings and the general low quality of the meetings themselves were especially horrifying under the circumstances, as when Dr. Tyler announced that 35 of the 50 state superintendents of public instruction were in that particular audience.

Quite a lot of wordage has been devoted to the White House Conference because it is significant as a bellwether for American education and will be for some time to come; and the media field, as a field or as a profession, came off badly. There were, it should be added, two positive factors—one supplied the briefcases for the participants, and Vice-President Humphrey gave educational media a plug in his speech. Basically, the. White House Conference must be seen as an expression of the new power structure in American education—the New Educational Establishment. If the National Education Association, the loose coalition of state education associations, the chief state social officers, professors of education generally, and the American Association of School Administrator continue to think of themselves as the Educational Establishment, they had better forget it. There is a New Educational Establishment, and what this power group thinks about educational media or audiovisual communication is absolutely crucial to the professional development of instructional technology. Therefore, the New Educational Establishment and its general attitude toward and performance with educational media needs further exploration as a major part of the negative side of the professional paradox. And there are other element, such as the absolutely decisive role of Jerrold Zachariass in media development, the disappearance of some of our old friends, the low condition of state-level audiovisual administration, the fundamental lack of understanding and support of our field among teacher and administrator organizations, etc.

Once these somewhat dismal factors have been explored in the next article—attention can be directed to the mixed and troublesome situation within the media profession itself. While we may not yet be in the position of appreciating our enemies more than our friends, we will probably get to that stage fairly soon Such incidents as the recent anti-intellectual memorandum submitted by the Audiovisual Education Association of California to the DAVI Delegate Assembly need to be scrutinized, as well as the state and nature of our training and certification programs, the national organization power struggle, the inability of the profession to develop standards, and the general commitment to footragging.

After the exasperating state of affairs within the profession of instructional technology is located with the paradox of success and failure, the problem will have been defined. It then may be possible, in the concluding article, to suggest new dimensions for the marginal media man and how these dimensions may be drawn All in all, it is an uncomfortable pattern of thinking that we face, but, if there is to be a salvation in media, it will be because we persisted with, as the sportswriters say, a hard nose.

A rather recent and somewhat extensive experience on the national level working with professors of several disciplines on the problem of using the newer educational media in their respective fields has developed what we believe to be a useful way of thinking about the application of media to college level instruction. Professors of various subjects approach these new instructional processes in several different ways, depending in general upon their degree of naivete and, to borrow a concept from Professor Burner the structure of their disciplines. Thus, geographers as a whole are very knowledgeable about a wide range of media because of the nature of geographic investigation, information storage, and communication; however, within the universe of geographers, there is a wide range of knowledge-ability and performance with media extending from unsophisticated to sophisticated. We have found historians, on the other hand, much less sophisticated in general in the media field, but with a great desire to learn about it, beginning at a performance level somewhat below that of geographers. This is due, we believe, to the nature of historical investigation, information storage, and communication.

With the concept as background, we ran turn to a classification media relationships in college instruction. In one sense, educational media used at the college and university level can be thought of as existing in several categories or levels. These are:

1. The tool level
2. The data level
3. The behavior control level
4. The meaning level
5. The research level
6. The systems level

The tool level

The tool level may be defined as providing the instructor with certain devices and materials with which he may do better what he is already accustomed to doing. The prime example of a tool-level device is the overhead transparency projector. In its simplest form, it is a much more efficient chalkboard; in a more sophisticated form using prepared transparencies, colored overlays, etc. It provides a lecturer with a powerful device. Other examples of tool-level devices are automatic slide projectors; semiautomatic photocopying devices; and individual single-room, closed-circuit television systems in which the system is operated by the instructor in lecture-demonstration situations. Characteristically, tool-level instructional technology is, at all times, under the direct control of the instructor, and the materials used are generally created by or for him.

The data level

This concept refers to the fact that information of all kinds is no longer stored exclusively in conventional print form. Data may be originally recorded on or transferred to various forms of photographic, magnetic or even thermoplastic storage. Microfiche cards, computer tapes, videotapes, high-speed motion pictures, audiotapes, and colored still pictures are among the many examples of media used in this manner. Obviously, such sources of information set new requirements for student assignments, "library"—type research, and the use of such information in the classroom situation. Devices of many kinds and different approaches to materials are required.

The behavior control level

Here we refer to the area known as programed instruction—considered broadly. It is a characteristic of all such programing that great energy is spent on a prior basis encoding the content into some form of program designed either to shape the behavior of the student on a controlled basis or to lead the student through carefully planned sequences of subject matter, branched or unbranched. The program material may appear in many forms—print, colored slides, 8 mm film loops, audio-tapes, etc. The language laboratory is a special case of this category. From the point of view of the instructor, the work is all done before contact with the student is made.

The meaning level

The term "meaning level" is used to describe the applicability of a wide range of educational media to the problem of building meaning into abstractions. In a simple case, a modem picture might be used to convey a certain amount of concrete background so that a student may build meaning into an abstraction Some college instructors argue that after a bright student has passed the age of five, you no longer "have to, show him pictures". This theory has two fundamental weaknesses, First, it assume's humans are equally at home in all fields and hence can be communicated with at a high-level of abstraction in all fields simply because they can manage verbal and mathematical symbols. This is simply not true. Secondly, it assumes that all humans learn in the same way through the same sequences of symbolic manipulation. In contrast, there is plenty of evidence, for example, that students vary even within a profile of listerning skills in a similar manner to the way they vary in reading skills, and that these two patterns do not match in the same individual.

Meaning, however, goes beyond grounded understanding of abstract symbols. There are affective, emotional characteristics. There is the world of the concrete, the flesh, *per se*. Here, again, the newer media permit the instructor to deal with affective meaning and the other dimensions of life on a controlled basis.

The research level

The research level is the complement of the data level. The only difference, really, is purpose and, time. Today, many forms of instrumentation are used in research to record, to measure, to observe. Much of this instrumentation is, in fact, communication technology applied to research instead of instruction. A phenomenon may be photographed at thousands of frames per second; dialects may be recorded; documents may be x-rayed. The list could go on, but the point is that the university faculty member doing research needs a range of media support merely to do his research. The ultimate results of such recording and measurement may eventually end up as "library" materials at the data level. Their generation, however, is a different function.

The systems level

An interesting tendency of the last decade has been a move toward the so-called systems approach to instruction. Generally, this has meant the creation of systems of instructional materials—books, manuals, recordings, films, programed materials, tests, etc.—covering an area of subject matter in a systematic way designed to achieve rather precise objectives. Computer-assisted instruction, when designed to cover whole courses or large segments of courses, is also referred to as an instructional system. In either case, the highly systematic design required presents a new level and use of media. At this point in time, the experimentation with instructional systems at the university level is not extensive, but there are signs that with the advent of Computer-assisted instruction, large-scale use of television, dial-access systems such as that now in operation at The Ohio State University, and similar approaches, a much more systematic use of media—perhaps at the whole course level—is in the offing. Again the implications for the instructional staff are the same as those appearing under the behavioural control-level concept; much of the activity of the instruction is prior to the instruction and, in the case of systems, also involved in the feedback-evaluation loop.

There are, as we all know, many ways to describe the elephant, and the category system just used cannot accomodate another media function relating particularly to higher education. Institutions of higher learning have, for the most part, extensive campuses: many of them house students as well as instruct them, so that the entire plant is spread out, and in it are performed many functions. Certain of the media can be viewed as transmission systems as well as processors of instruction. Television, audio lines, low-grade signal lines, and computer links are examples. All of these can be used to connect the separate units of the physical plant and transmit mediated instruction throughout.

It follows that any concern with media on a university campus should take into account this possibility. Recently, for example, in the midwest, dormitories are being connected with the central closed-circuit television system, and instruction is reaching students in the housing areas. This is also true of dial-access audio instruction. For university functions, the newer educational media can be applied at several levels—as individiual instructional tools, as data storage, for behavior control-type instruction, to build meaning; as research tools, as the core of instructional systems, and as means to increase the distribution efficiency of learning experiences of all kinds. If available, the individual university faculty member can select one or more of these levels at any time.

Educational innovation

It is within this general context of the development and present state of the art of educational media that the remainder of this paper will consider Title III. Basic to this consideration was the detailed examination of approximately 40 proposals of various types which had been funded under the initial Title III grants and a site visit to a California school district which had begun operation under a Title III innovative grant.

The writers had to struggle with a form which was obviously put together by the same committee that created the camel. The most fundamental problem, however, is the fact that Title III has two parts—almost equal and opposite. Even more confusing, when one of the parts is analyzed, it too has, potentially two parts. The first part of Title III, as everyone must know by this time, provides for the formation of supplementary educational service centers on some sort of regional basis. Within this provision, however, are traditional services which are often not available or not sufficiently available to schools—guidance, health, media, etc.—plus central services embracing art, music, dance, etc. While to a legislator or to an abstract organization administrator such a conglomeration seems reasonable, from the point of view of the realities of the educational system as it exists, these are two kettles and they both don't even contain fish. In the stated objectives of the proposals which analyzed, objectives relating to cultural services were dragged in by the heels in order that the proposal might be kosher and obtain other needed services for the district.

The Second part of Title III is variously referred to as innovative, exemplary, demonstrative. It is to provide funds for program which develop innovations and exemplary program. Obviously, such programs would have different objectives from those for supplementary service centers. They did not, in many cases. Again, the cultural elements plus unreal service objectives showed up in the proposals. Whether the proposers could not read or whether they were touching all bases just to be safe come to mind as alternatives causing this objective mishmash.

There were a few cases of this, at least in part, but mainly the real objectives were buried among a pile of irrelevant baggage. Hence, in many cases, the program was not related to a portion of the objectives as stated in the proposals. Programms did not seem, however, to be well related to the real objectives—stated or unstated.

So much for objectives. Since the main thrust of Title III for the present is to be in the direction of educational innovation with its concomitant functions of example and dissemination of results, it would be useful to continue this discussion of the proposals with some analysis of the problem of educational innovation as it relates to Title III. Some years ago, Hoban pointed out that the agricultural model for innovation probably did not apply to education, since education was a bureaucracy and that no one really knew very much about innovation in a bureaucracy. Act Wally, the way Title III operates with the proposal generating within a local bureaucracy and with one copy going to the State Educational Agency—another bureaucracy—and the final award being given by the U.S. Office of Education, after due cognizance of the state reaction, we have here an attempt at educational innovation within bureaucracy cubed.

Now there may be nothing wrong with this procedure providing certain realistic views are taken of the whole process. The question has been continually raised, 'Were the proposals reviewed really innovative?" This problem has been well discussed among members of the task force and, of course, the answer has to be, "Innovative for Whom?" In the field of educational technology, almost every possibility discussed above has been experimented with somewhere, and, in that sense, unless we are considering a proposal to use broadcasts from Telstar, or lasers as information trasmitters, or ESP, nothing is likely to be strictly speaking, innovative in the Kuhn sense of creating a new pafadigm never before set forth.

At a level slightly below this, however, there is a field for innovation that goes beyond something merely new locally. For example, the library learning centers being installed at Temple City, California, are, in fact, quite a new concept even though a portion of the setup is in the classification of audiovisual access systems for individual students forms of which are being experimented with at several places in the United States. Educational innovation, then, in my view, cannot be classified either as something completely new or something that is only new within the locality or region Rather, it should be thought of as existing on a continuum.

If the concept of an innovative continuum is acceptable, obviously the judgements required of the Title III staff must be more discriminating if the avowed effort is to encourage innovation somewhere in the abstract as opposed to innovation within the local environment. These proposals tended to be oriented to individualized learning, computer utilization, and various forms of dial-access systems with some attention to television. This merely reflects the "in" elements of instructional technology as of the fall of 1966.

On the other hand, one proposal dealt with filming certain teaching practices which could then be used as media for inservice and preservice education of teachers.

It was claimed in the proposal that the practices to be filmed themselves were innovative, but the major effort of the proposal was for the filming—hardly a new idea, yet bound to produce useful and new material if done properly. This project would have to be rated as noninnovative; however, if the film proved useful and the practices were new, the films could be used all over the country and would be presenting an innovation.

It is when we come to the supplementary service centers that received operational grants that the question of innovation gets in the way. Many school systems lack new media and equipment and the logistics support to apply them to instruction. Help—great deal of help—is needed. Two of the proposals examined were from one or more country units literally thousands of miles apart. Both had the same problem—they had nothing in the way of new media and needed toolingg up even to reach a minimum Both felt they had to justify their proposals on the grounds of innovation and went through some twisting and turning in the writing in order to prove this. Both were innovating locally, but, more than that, they were improving instruction and relating their programs to the modern world. It seems to me that no more justification is needed. In one case involving two countries with 23 school districts in an isolated area of a northwestern state, the annual expenditure for audiovisual materials to service about 12,000 students amounted, on a three-year average, to about $ 5,500 per year. Innovation might be nice, but a much better technological base is a necessity for these two countries.

This brings up two related aspects of this problem that should be considered. Both are concerned with instructional technology and innovation. These two aspects of the problem are:

1. The claim that proposing districts or other entities

are requesting too much money for equipment and materials.

2. The claim that curriculum development is much more important than any effort to do anything about instructional technology.

In the case of the first claim, one of the major functions of a technological society is innovation through technology—so why not through instructional technology?. The implication of this claim is that, somehow, tooling up is a second-rate approach to innovation, probably more influenced by projector salesmen or TV peddlers than educational objectives. These, assumptions behind this claim are based on the old-fashioned view, discussed above, that technology is a "thine, not a process function. It is highly likely that an infusion of technology will institute more change per dollar spent than all curriculum meetings, inservice education bashes, and professional library book purchases a district could generate during twice the period covered. There is a further overtone of that same educational puritanism here which Anna Hyer once described as the philosophy of new uses for old coat hangers. Such puritanism is neither efficient nor in gear with any kind of modern economic thinking.

In the site visit made, the superintendent was questioned closely with regard to the genesis of his project. His point was that he had spotted a very great need and could see no other solution to meet it than to come up with a new technological system—which he did. The need was for a certain kind of individualized instruction and the solution was to develop a highly technologized learning center adjacent to the library. He is now finding that other innovations are occuring as a result of this capability and he and his staff are busy generating proposals to both public and private sources for further development. The second claim that curriculum development is more important than technological development is, first of all, the direct result of the "addendum" viewpoint referred to in the introductory section. More important, it is completely out of touch with reality. One only needs to look at the great curriculum revision projects that now occupy the national scene. With the exception of one or two, such as Project English, the entire curriculum reform movement is accomplishing its objectives through instructional technology.

Many years ago, Dale and Corey reminded the audiovisual field that what children do in school is usually a consequence of the instructional materials used by the teacher. This is Professor Zacharias' main credo. Once the content has been set to satisfaction of the experts in the discipline, it is converted to educational media—films, paperbacks, programed instruction, etc.—and moved into the schools via these vehicles. This is true curriculum reform because what the students do is now totally changed. It would be well for those making Title III policy to study this lesson very carefully. All of this argument suggests that educational technology is, perhaps, the best possible machine for instituting the changes thought desirable. Even if this idea were accepted, 'certain roadblocks remain that show up in the proposals from certain states with strong educational bureaucracies. Although the law provides that the proposing entity applies directly to the federal government, a copy must go the state agency and be reacted to. In strong states, it is possible for these agencies to, in fact, control this process through state regulations, pressures, etc. In California, for example, there is sort of an unwritten, oral requirement that all proposals must contain statements of behavioral objectives. The assumption seems to be that the success of all innovation hinges on the acceptance of Skinnerian theory. This would be a hard case to make.

In New York there are rumblings about the controls existing through regional committees controlled by the state. The problem here is that innovation is difficult at best; under vigorous bureaucratic control it may be well nigh impossible. The state bureaucracies, however, through controlling the proposals, have an efficient means of controlling the direction of new developments in their states while, at the same time, piously claiming local autonomy. As one superintendent put it, "...the trick is to nurture creativity at the local level". Nurture and control are two different things.

Both at the federal level and at the state levels, we are attempting through Title III to institutionalize educational innovation through bureaucracies, further, when dealing these days with cities of any size, we have to add a third bureaucratic level with much greater controls than both other levels put together. It is still a very moot point whether or not bureaucracy is the exact opposite of innovation. Apparently it needn't be; all of the proposals examined had some elements of innovation, existing somewhere upon the continuum. Time will tell as to the extent, lasting power, and future generating power of these innovative efforts sitting, as they do, within bureaucracy cubbed.

There are some other notes that ought to be made in this somewhat rambling discussion of the proposals. Questions were raised with the task force as to the scholarly elements the proposals contained. "Did they,' for example, "indicate a reasonable familiarity with the literature?" Frankly, they did not. The best proposal from the point of view of sheer innovative power, also contained the best literature backup. Many of the supplementary center proposals indicated no literature work-up whatsoever. The condition of the proposals does suggest that, for the planning grants, the subsequent operational proposals should be scrutinized more carefully for literature familiarity due to the fact that time has been available for an adequate search.

With the exception of one or two units that were located near or were cooperating with higher institutions, very little was said about evaluation in the proposals examined.

We can turn, then, to the question as to the provisions for dissemination of the results of the innovative efforts as they come to pass. There were some modest efforts to provide for dissemination in some of the proposals; by far the best was a plan submitted by a country in southern Illinois to use television as an instrument for dissemination. In general, however, dissemination plans were weak or nonexistent. Many of the weak ones proposed the same old thing of teachers' meeting, attendance at courses, etc. with, perhaps, a mention of a newspaper story or two.

The entire American educational community would hardly take first prize for its dissemination activities—and this particularly includes the U.S. Office of Education and most state departments. No doubt legislative restrictions play a part in this, but that cannot be the only reason. The U.S. Office of Education has funds and a unit designed to disseminate the results of research and other information; its greatest achievement to date is to come up with the beginning of what will probably be a very good information storage and retrieval system for research information. However, an information storage and retrieval system is not a dissemination machine; it is the fuel for such a machine. The machine does not exist and, if the innovative reports from Title III go into ERIC under the theory that they will then be disseminated, the most we can say is that we have given them a more decent burial than is usual for such documents. There was nothing particularly useful, let alone spectacular, in the proposals concerning dissemination: I see nothing at either the state or federal levels which will compensate for this. Dissemination remains a major problem.

Finally, we were asked to comment on weaknesses or gaps which showed up in the proposals other than those already discussed. With respect to those proposals dealing with educational media, I founded four:

1. Manpower
2. Lack of adequate consultants
3. A relatively naive attitude toward production problems and an unrealistic treatment of production problems, including budgeting
4. Requests for advanced technology without an adequate technological base, including the all-important logistical support.

Of these weaknesses or gaps, the manpower problem is the most serious. There is today, as noted above, a very grave shortage of qualified manpower in the educational media field.

When technology is applied on any reasonable scale and at some depth, specialized manpower is required. Further, if modem views of the technological function in education are accepted, the key types of manpower needed are in the design-engineering consultant area. Other types, of course, are also needed, principally technical administrators and technical specialists ranging from television producers through graphic artists to electronic technicians. Perhaps the greatest problem faced by those charged with making all Title III proposals operate successfully is to recruit the specialized manpower required from a Minimum, Poverty-stricken market If the slots cannot be filled with the poverty qualified people, they will 'be filled with unqualified or minimally qualified personnel—and the whole program will be in jeopardy.

The second gap noticed was, in many cases, the lack of adequate consultants available to the proposers during the process of developing the proposal. Several proposals embraced rather sophisticated technological approaches, but had, apparently, no outside expert consultants, and insufficient, attention was paid to providing for them in the proposal itself.

Some of the better proposals, on the other hand, made use of a locally developed expertise and definitely reflected that expertise. For example, a group of school districts in Texas associated themselves with a sophisticated local university computer center, and this excellent proposal reflected this thinking. Experts do not have to come from thousands of miles away, but they ought to be experts.

Relating to the consultant problem, perhaps a note should be added on the anti-commercialisation syndrome that exists, to some degree, subrosa in the U.S. Office of Education. This view is certainly legitimate in many cases it is expressed in the general worry that the substantial parts of many proposals are written, not by qualified educational experts, but by salesmen working on a commission for some audiovisual dealer or book peddler—with all that implies in terms of unnecessary equipment, etc. etc. Some of the time this is no doubt true. In the proposals examined, however, where the fine hand of commercialism was detected as it was in perhaps 10 percent of the lot—the proposals were still good.

The issue here has to be, not where did the advice come from, but was it competent? There are many well-qualified commercial representatives calling on schools.

In other cases, the salesman-consultant represents every bad sterotype that haunts, the somewhat puritanical educational frame of refererce-including elevator shoes.

In the third place, most proposals and committees generating proposals that we have contacted take a very naive view of the problems inherent in generating new materials of any kind. For example, one proposal intends to use teachers to prepare a certain kind of "program". Even though some provision was made for time off, etc., and it was stated that the teachers concerned were somewhat experienced in preparing such materials.. It takes much more time, effort, energy, skill, and know-how to produce an extensive range of educational materials than was provided. This gap—or deficiency—was present in many proposals. A dial—access system for audiotapes is of little use if all of the tapes are to be prepared locally or copied surreptitiously from phonograph records or other tapes using extra teacher time.

The point is not so much the old hardware-software problem so often expounded on in recent pronouncements. Rather it is that adequate provisions in terms of manpower, facilities, and time must be made available in generous amounts in order to do the job of producing new software. It takes much longer and requires much more effort than the proposers seem to think. There is another important sidebar here. Based on the outmoded theories referred to above, many school administrators feel that it is somehow immoral to provide time off for teachers to do these jobs or to pay for substitutes or to provide extra compensation or to set the teacher up on a separate simmer salary in order to create new materials. It is true that such provisions have been and are being made in many places, but it is my feeling that the majority of administrators still feel that such extra work, may be, extracted out of the "professional contribution hide of the dedicated teacher Proposals need to be carefully scrutinized from this point of view. We are skirting the edge of a teacher revolt in this country anyway, and the effort to innovate should not contribute to it. The last gap or deficiency that needs to be explored is revealed in the fact that some of the proposals examined and others, no doubt, furnished other members of the task force—are designed to develop a sophisticated technology upon an almost nonexistent technological base. A final suggestion might be made about a gap that is not so much a gap, but a possible illusion. Dr. Thomas James, dean of the School of Education at Stanford, recently commented in a search in Los Angeles that much of the alleged innovation that was going on—particularly that relating to educational technology—was more or less a fake. James' idea seemed to be that districts were engaging in so-called innovative practices because federal or state funds were available, that once these funds disappeared, the machines would go on the closet shelf, dust would gather on the materials, and the districts would go back to older, more comfortable, and certainly less expensive ways. While I do not go along with Dr. James all the way, he has a point. There is, I think, some of this feeling abroad in school administration circles today. This superficial frosting of innovative practices on the old school cake, if really true, represents not so much a possible a gap but a potential reversal of the whole innovative business. This may be a serious matter and should be teated as such by the Title III staff.

Recommendations

1. Instructional technology be viewed as defined in this paper—a complex pattern of man-machine systems and organizations based on concepts of feasibility and that proposals centering on hardware and materials be required to show some understanding

of this concept on an operational basis. This is to say that the proposals' cannot treat hardware and/or materials in isolation from the more complex technological process.

2. In connection with Number 1, a complete and workable logistical pattern be required in every proposal centering on a technological approach to instruction.
3. The proposing institution be required to describe in detail the technological base upon which it is intended to install new technology.
4. The proposing institution be required to show the consultants used in preparing the proposal and the consultants it is intended to use in carrying out the project. This description of the consultants should be so designed so as to establish their competency and no consultant should be considered incompetent solely on the basis of the position he holds whether that position be commercial, educational or religious.

   The proposing institution be required to show precisely where it intends to obtain its technological manpower and to establish some competency for this manpower.

6. Where production of any kind of audiovisual or programed material is contemplated, the readers be cautioned to examine carefully the provisions of the proposal fox this production. They are to specifically look at budgetary, manpower and time arrangements along the lines suggested in the main body of the paper. Generally, they are to avoid underfinanced and unrealistic approaches to production. If a proposal has merit and is not properly set up for this function, care should be exercised by the Title III staff that the proper support is provided in the negotiations.

7. Detailed equipment and material lists be eliminated from the proposals.
8. A panel of media experts be convened to set up evaluate standards for the states to use in reacting to media proposals. If the states desire to add additional reactions, they should be required to state very clearly, in operational terms, what additional criteria they are using.
9. The Title III administration, since it is investing in the tooling up of American education, begin immediately to press for standards, first for equipment. It is suggested that this might be done through a university or similar institution working with concerned groups, as, for example, the Educational Media Council, the Department of Audiovisual Instruction of the NEA, the National Association of Educational Broadcasters, and the related commercial, industrial and professional groups such as the Society of Motion Picture and Television Engineers. Every effort ought to be made to begin this program at once and attempt to schedule its completion in two or three years. As standards become available, they should be included in the guidelines of proposal readers.
10. Some Title III money be made available, either through the Title XI (NDEA) program, the Title VI-B program, the experienced teacher fellow ship program, and/or Title III itself to improve the manpower situation in the media field. Programs of some length designed to retread general school administrators, update conventional media personnel, and, particularly, to recruit new people are badly needed. It may be that money could be put into award; for projects which would provide for extensive training of school personnel already involved in the projects. This training level ought,

due to the general situation in education, be at the advanced masters degree level.

11. The Title III staff immediately initiate studies of dissemination and the relationship of information to behavior change Further these studies should be oriented to using communication technology to carry out this dissemination.

Perhaps it might be useful to summarize Mr. Muller's reader can certain understand arguments, although any well-written exposition The them from his clear and summary will however, assist in delivering the reaction. Essentially, Mr Muller argues that educational technology has been oversold at every point, along the line and has had little if any real effect on the educational enterprise; that people, not technology, can provide better education; that technology can never solve our basic problems; and that the computer can make three contributions to instruction: (a) through computer-managed instruction, (b) through providing the computer to the students so that he may manipulate data and thereby learn thought processes, logic, etc., and (c) through Providing direct instruction in the use of data processing and computer equipment both as vocational training and for general education.

There certainly little to quarrel with concerning these three potential uses of the computer. We would agree that CAI has been oversold in certain quarters, up to and including the Bureau of Research of the U.S. Office of Education. This is not to say, however, that the potential is not there probably 10 to 20 years in the future. The trick, of course, is to figure what potential. It would have been helpful if Muller had engaged in some speculation on this point.

However, one cannot discuss education and the new technology and concentrate on three relatively peripheral uses of the computer—that is, one cannot do it when, in the introductory pages of the paper the whole philosophical problem of technology and education is raised and examined. Such a stance rather requires showing a more thorough understanding of the vast range of technological devices, materials, patterns of organization, and systems relating to education than Mr. Muller presented.

Muller presented, for example, a quote from Dean Sizer of Harvard that appeared in his report to the president to the effect that the large companies that had recently entered the field of education had backed off because the school system is both broke and conservative.

Many things have been involved in these abortive adventures including, for example, some cases of incredibly bad management, demands to turn a profit in 12 to 18 months, the whole theory of conglomerate management which is very reluctant to integrate its own divisions in new Projects when they sit making profits the way they are, the unbelievable conservatism of the Publishing companies, in this country—some of them may not Yet be using movable type, the lack of a viable marketing organization, and so on.

We need, perhaps, a little less "high-flying rhetoric" concerning both the promises and accomplishments and the failures and dangers of technology in education. We can no longer afford these Ciceronian luxuries; unbounded and unquestioned enthusiasm for this or that bit of instructional technology on the one hand or a failure of nerve in the face of the problems of technological development in education on the other are both conditions under which the cement of the educational status quo will harden until it cracks into bits that will have to be swept up by the societal broom. The medicine man promises of technological panaceas for education will only, as Mr. Muller indicates, result in regression and retreat on the part of the educational community when the hopes that have been aroused meet the hard-nosed reality of the confounding educational system. The failure of nerve will bring about the same result in that it will amplify the inertia of both the professionals and public bodies that comprise the system in the face of the exacting and difficult task of technological development in education As the inertia increases, the system will fall apart. Such is the penalty of failure of nerve.

The Muller paper reflects a line of thinking that we believe to be both pessimistic and one-sided. The genesis of this line of thinking, as well as its opposite—the "2mm filmstrip will save American education for the Indians' type—lies in the fact that many commentators since about 1958 who have chosen to speak about educational technology do not know the business. They do not know the business in the sense that they did not sweat through the scrambling visual-audiovisual movement into television, programmed instruction, and multi-screen, multimedia techniques and face the sunset looking at computers, simulators and probably holographic lasers useful in conveying patterns of ESP.

Perhaps there's a little dramatic license here, but not much. The pronouncements on educational technology come and go—exceedingly optimistic to gloomily pessimistic—often unrelated to the infinite realities of the educational system and the possibilities of instructional technology, and, at best, concentrating on experimental results or under funded developments. The overcautious pessimistic view of technology in general and instructional technology in particular tends to come, in my opinion, from two postures. They are (1) the literary side of the Snowian dichotomy of the two cultures—

science and literature, and (2) an anachronistic puritanism toward business, etc. which continues to pervade the ranks of public education. I would not put either Mr. Muller or Dean Sizer in the second category, but I believe them to be excellent representatives of the first.

To clinch this point, I should like to quote Sir Robert Watson-Watt, the father of radar and one of the originators of operations research. In a conference sponsored by the Center for the Study of Democratic Institutions at which he was definitely in the minority, he had this to say:

> Because I suspect some here of sharing Ellul's pessimism., I am moved to comment very personally—with appropriate apologies—on the imbalance of judgement which is almost inevitable between those who have been brought up mainly on a diet of printed paper, and those nurtured on wood shavings, iron and brass fillings, propulsive gases and other base mechanic offal. *It is quite clear to me that pessimism is nurtured by paper, optimism by offal of the kind I have just mentioned.*

The business of knowing or not, knowing the business of educational technology is illustrated by Muller's rapid generalizations concerning the history of the claims for a series of technological devices when they were introduced into education and his conclusion that the influence of these devices has been marginal—without assessing the milieu in which the exaggerated claims were stated. Thus, he says that similar claims were made for radio in the 20s, film in the 30s, television in the 50s, and computers in the 60s. Actually, we have old Thomas Edison to blame for exaggeration in the case of films. He said much the same thing several times, but here is an authenticated statement which appeared in the *New York Dramatic Mirror's* issue of July 9, 1913:

> Books will soon be obsolete in the schools. Scholars will soon be instructed through the eye. It is possible to teach every branch of human knowledge with the motion picture. Our school system will be completely changed in ten years.

We can turn now to the 30s, the period Muller states was the time in which the claim was generally made that films would revolutionize education. The best book on the subject covering the 30s came out in 1942. Consider these two experts from this report covering four years of experimentation by the Motion Picture of the American Council on Education.

> The fact that motion pictures are a pictorial language with a universal appeal, that they arouse a wide variety of student interests, that students of varying mental maturity respond to them in characteristically different ways, and that faulty concepts and superficial Understanding sometimes develop from films has important implications for the curriculum.

It is the function of motion pictures to provide Pictorial representation of the "sensible world", and it is the function of the teacher, with the aid of the book and the lecture, the laboratory and the discuss ion group, the library and the study Period, to direct and guide the student in "penetrating within" in order to find substantial reality", "meaning," and "truth".

No doubt there were salesmen that were making extravagant statements during the 30s about films in education, but responsible comment on films and education during that crucial decade followed the Hoban line. The audiovisualist, then—as the instructional technologist, now—occupied the grey land between the white and black mountains of irresponsible rhetoric and stygian inertia—admittedly a little closer to optimism than pessimism.

Mr. Muller introduced the concept of irresponsible rhetoric making high-blown, unacceptable claims as to the value and usefulness of this or that technology in education only to be folllowed by disappointment in the educational community. Admittedly, we have had some of these claims and the effects on the educational community Mr. Muller suggests since the scanty beginnings of an educational technology. A man by the name of Josiah F. Bumstead in a book on the blackboard in 1841 stated:

> The inventor or introducer of the blackboard system deserves to be ranked among the best contributors to learning and science, if not among the greatest benefactors of mankind.

It would be more useful to consider educational claims of all kinds as a general phenomena, occuring at a given time in the technological development process, set within a given technological milieu and complex of attitudes, training levels, and political-social forces existing within the educational system, and uttered by a particular class of educator or promoter. Care is needed to assess the source of the claims and the effective response of the educational system, if any, particularly by comparison with what was said and done by that small band of instructional technologists who were actually in the business at the time. Such a study would, I think, be of great assistance in helping design educational technology for the future. A few tentative suggestions as to answers may be made in the hope that this phenomena might be investigated thoroughly at a later time.

For example, the tentative idea could be advanced that people close to the initial invention or development of a device or system such as the motion picture would have a sudden shock of recognition and project claims for beyond the ability of the times to carry them out, the educational system to absorb them, or even the primitive state of the technology to deliver. This would account far Edison's claims. And here is another example. In January 1933, Professor E.B. Kurtz, Head of the Department of Electrical Engineering of the State University of Iowa, and his colleagues successfully began broadcasting educational television programs. On the occasion of inauguration of the second series of educational broadcasts

> ... this new instrumentality, which bids fair to become the most potent agency for universal education ever conceived. For in due time, every home will have its own classroom, with professor, blackboard, diagrams, pictures, and students.

Note that this is about as far back in time from the claims for television in the 50s as Edison's remarks were from the claims for ill in the 30s. Accepting for the moment the shock of recognition idea on the part of the inventor or pioneer developer, our tentative exploration can now enter another area—that of the educational leader and his role in prophecy or claim. Casual observation suggests that somewhere along the line certain farsighted educational leaders pick up the ball and make public pronouncements far in advance of educational thinking that receive a certain amount of currency—even if not acceptance in the form of action. In this connection, I find four quotations fascinating:

> ... George F. Zook, in his report to the American Council on Education in 1940, described the motion picture as "the most revolutionary instrument introduced in education since the printing press."

> Dr. Thomas Clark Pollock of New York University said more recently, "It now seems clear, however, that television offers the greatest opportunity for the advancement of education since the introduction of printing by movable type".

> "It is the first major technological innovation in education since the development of printing."

> "The impact of the computer on society, and hence on the curriculum, has been compared to that of movable type and the printing press since Gutenberg."

Mr. Muller may feel that I have uncovered enough to document his entire argument. I believe otherwise-that such claims at the leadership level are a part of a leading process and, in the time stage in which they are made, merely get the idea into the broader system, giving it currency. Effects on practice at that point are inconsequential, and expectations at that same point are only slightly stimulated. In fact, as is well known in the case of television, the efforts of the Ford Foundation produced more of a "Ho-hum, what else is new?" attitude than anything else.

Somewhere between initial recognition and the prophetic public statements of certain educational leaders, work by the technologists has begun. Ideas have been picked up and laboratory or field development started. Here, again, the description of this process would be well worth the effort to dig it out. This will not be easy because, for example, there is the phenomena of false starts which are revived later and which must be taken into account. The nitty-gritty of technological development may remain more or less unnoticed by the educational community, or experimental centers may become more public relations demonstration arrangements than true developmental efforts.

Since educational technology usually involves some kind of product—hardware or software the possibilities of commercial exploration are always present. This results, sometimes after development begins, in various enterprises that may or may not succeed, but which contact the educational community and spread the word, unfortunately often in the extravagant sense noted by Mr. Muller. However, in all fairness, it should be pointed out that industrial representatives have, also, in many cases done an excellent, professional job of dissemination of information on technological developments and have helped teachers and others at the grass roots level with problems of using the new technology.

Before proceeding with the end of the tale of reaching the educational community and discussing the community's response, it is necessary to note that changes in this process have occurred in the last few years. Today, for example, with the larger corporations, at least, market research is conducted to determine whether or not the company should enter the "knowledge business." Research and development on new devices, materials, processes, and systems is much more programmatic, being funded principally from federal sources; large industry, too, is investing slightly more in research and development in educational technology. These processes will, no doubt, change the fundamental flow of discovery, invention, development, and adoption. Whether or not it will change the process of claiming is open to question.

It should also be noted that—as part of a general, though weak, programmatic attack on the problems of education which moves the whole process away from the older, laissez faire approach—educational innovation is (a) being studied itself in order to develop an applied science, and (b) the process of innovation is being formalized and encouraged by federal law and state action in the form of, for example, the Title III innovative centers set up under the provisions of the Elementary and Secondary Education Act. The second development, of course, is designed deliberately to encourage dissemination of information about new developments, many of which fall into the classification of educational technology. These deliberate processes, though, run exactly contrary to the extravagant claim situation—insofar as educators and research workers play a part in it—as the system emphasizes evaluation and caution. Returning now to the response of the educational community, eventually adoption, assimilation and vulgarization of the processes, materials, devices, and even organization patterns occur. Although the subject of much study in recent years by Rogers and others, the innovative-adoptive process remains essentially a mystery in which a crystall ball is as useful a predictor as statements of the characteristics of "early' and "late" adopters.

The response of the educational system to technological development is another crucial point in the Muller paper. To repeat, he indicates that instructional technology, to this point in time, has had only a marginal effect upon the system.

Some data on these matters do exist In addition to the baseline data generated by the Finn, Perrin and Campion study cited above, the studies of Eleanor P. Godfrey and the Bureau of Social Science Research on the state of audiovisual technology in the first half of this decade are" especially illuminating when the question of "marginal effect" is raised. Were, for example, the estimated 7,000,000 filmstrips on hand in the public schools in *1961* marginal or something more?

The key item in the Godfrey studies, however, was the comparison made on her sample for *1961* and *1964*. In this connection, she says:

> Some of the individual gains were quite spectacular: increases of 12, 10, 9 and 7 units per school were reported for tape recorders, record players, television sets, and overhead projectors.

As a result of the general increase in amount of equipment per school, the median inventory *level* shifted upward for art items except radio, where the level remained constant at one unit per school over the three-year period. In 1964, assuming that he had all nine equipment items, the superintendent of the hypothetical median district had one overhead projetor for each two schools, seven television sets for each ten schools, two language laboratories for three secondary schools, two opaque projectors for every three schools, one radio in each building, and enough tape recorders, 16 mm projectors, slide-filmstrip, projectors, and record players to put one unit in every school and multiple units in some, presumably the larger ones.

Another soucre of comparative data is presented by two studies covering the status and growth of closed-circuit television in 1962 and 1967. As Jogenson indicated in the preface to the 1967 study:

> In 1962, the NEA's Technological Development Project's study of the status of closed-circuit television conducted that CCTV would "move forward at an accelerating pace during the next decade." It had identified 462 CCTV installations in 403 institutions. It is apparent at this halfway point in the decade that the prediction was accurate. Four years later the number of institutions reporting CCTV installations in the present survey has nearly doubled. Seven hundred and seventeen institutions now report 812 systems. An additional 178 institutions indicate they operate CCTV and/or ITFS systems or would do so by January 1968 although they did not respond to follow up inquiries. Taking these two figures in combination, it is fair to estimate that approximately 1,000 CCTV or ITFS systems will be in operation by 1968.

In the field of computers in higher education, Caffrey and Mosmann, using an earlier study by the

National Science Foundation and Information from an annual administrative data-processing survey among colleges and universities, state:

> ... More than 30 per cent of American colleges now use computers of some kind. In recent years, 80 to 100 institutions acquired their first computer each year... The number of computers installed at colleges increases at the rate of 45 per cent each year.

These computers, of course, are used for a variety of purposes, but they must be having some educational effect. A recent report by the NEA Research Division using a carefully controlled sample of 1,609 teachers throughout the country shows that from approximately 80 to 95 per cent report the availability of what we call conventional audiovisual devices and materials—still and motion projectors, audio devices etc. The more exotic devices for "newer media" CCTV, CAI and multimedia devices, as well as programmed instruction fall in much lower ranges. What is seen is a profile of availability. Even recognizing this, influence cannot really be measured.

Current technological development in education is obviously not yet equal to the task and demands that are being made upon it. Nonetheless, it is, I think, much more than marginal. In addition, it bears an importance that is sometimes missed. This argument, together with the data to support it, was developed some years ago when, as part of the 'of the Technological Development project' of the NEA, we did a study of the growth patterns in the acquisition of audiovisual equipment by the public schools from 1930 to 1960. Analysis of the data suggested that Rostow's concepts of the five stages of economic growth could be applied to the American school system and that the system could be thought of as a primitive or underdeveloped culture from a technological point of view. It then followed that

Rostow's conditions for take-off into a modem technological culture would apply. At that time:

> Prior to 1930, there was little in the form of communication equipment available to education. The growth patterns of acquisition then take on additional significance, as they reflect the general communication revolution as it entered education. The main Point, however, is that *we view the build-up* of *audiovisual* equipment and materials in education as one of principal preconditions for a technological revolution in education—for takeoff in the Rostow sense.
>
> The level this growth has attained and the speed and pattern of attainment are, we think, the best indicators of the future. Judgment has to be applied to the data in order to estimate whether or not the take-off point has been reached. It is clear, however, that, for example, the psychological preparation—the expectation and aspiration for technological solutions to educational problems—cannot exist until a technological *milieu* exists to create this preparation. The extent to which audiovisual equipment is available to the working school teacher is a valid test of the strength of the milieu. If for example, teaching machines or the electronic learning laboratory take the educational system by sotrm, it may be due more to the widespread availability of the 16mm sound motion picture Projector than all of the theories and research of experimental psychologists, the efforts of industry or the thousands, of words and pictures appearing in the mass media.

Since that time, the technological capital of the American school system has increased markedly due to the infusion of federal funds, changed attitudes on the part of educators, and the pressures of problems such as those generated in the inner city. It should be emphasized that the educational system is still highly underdeveloped technologically, but one would maintain that the present technological buildup, which is somewhat more than marginal in its effect, has provided a sufficient base for takeoff. In other words, we are farther along the line than Muller envisions without yet reaching a dollar volume which would encourage General Electric to bid on computer-assisted instruction for the state of Iowa rather than trying to catch a Navy contract for a flying submarine.

As sort of a corollary to his analysis of the claims—effects relationship of educational technology, Mr. Muller shifts the discussion temporarily to the effects of the mass media on children outside of school. This, he admits—with a passing reference to McLuhan—is considerable, and then he proceeds to the somewhat hoary issue of whether or not the machine will replace the teacher.

The machine—teacher question is handled by Muller with the sentence, "Our traditional education system will endure, and our teachers will teach—and our computers will never be a substitute". This is followed by a comment that only people and not machines can provide better education.

If one is sensitive to all of the recent account of ghetto and poverty-rural education and the traditional educational system operating therein, all one can upon reading Mr. Muller's sentence is to invoke the Deity for the country and take to the hills. It was no accident, for example, that a Black Power group in Los Angeles recently approached the principal of Manual Arts High School with a demand that several teachers be dismissed—*on the grounds that they were totally insensitive.* In any large city in the United States today, a neat question can be raised as to how many *human teaching machines* are in service. This concept, of course, is only a small chunk of the teachermachinechild relationship, The general issue has been widely discussed, and, no doubt, most readers are familiar with the arguments. The literature on differential staffing and discussions of proper roles of several levels of educational personnel within an organization structure that permits the use of a technology of instruction wherever it is applicable. Further, it was no accident that the great curriculum reform projects of this decade elected to use films, film loops, television, etc., to "preserve the integrity of the content". It appears that, as Professor Zacharias has said many times, children are also entitled to the truth.

Basically, with the population explosion, knowledge explosions and the great, inchoate revolutionary drive by all suppressed peoples for a place in the sun, we can no longer afford the luxury of the traditional system; that the system needs a vast overhaul and, in order to solve some of the problems presented by the three revolutions, we must develop a technology of education that will carry a greater share of the load than the simple idea that the teacher may be helped out a little now and then by some kind of an aid. Those designing education for the future must keep this in mind.

Two other reactions to this general problem should be mentioned. First, if technology applied to instruction does, assist in making differential staffing possible, it is not too clear as yet what master teachers or leading teachers of one kind or another are supposed to do. These actions are still clothed in broad generalizations such as "guidance", "individual attention," etc.

Secondly, everyone seem to be forgetting the teachers themselves within this whole picture of the teacher-machine relationship. This seems peculiar in a year that has been filled with teachers' strikes, militancy and hard-nosed negotiation. One of the great issues of the future as far as the educational technology is concerned is the role that teachers' organizations will play in its adoption through negotiation. The day of the arbitrary decision on the part of boards and administrators in many fields of education is fast coming to an end. The open question is: Will or will not teachers take a Luddite position?.

Leaving the teacher-machine-child question, we can briefly look at the other key question raised by the Muller paper. This question is concerned with the whole issue of the technological society and its effect on human beings. I am very much in sympathy with Mr. Muller at this point: He properly notes the generalized fear of standardization and conformity which a culture organized around a high technology generates with its punched cards, data banks, bureaucratic and organizational systems, and alienation of the person He claims that the key questions of the social order—tolerance or bigotry, for example—have, no technological solutions. The alternatives, of course, are ethical solutions. The situation is probably very mixed, but such a general hypothesis must, of necessity, be drastically revised if it can be shown that some problems of this nature have been resolved or partially resolved by technological means as opposed to ethical means.

Gerard Piel calls our attention to one such case—the case of slavery. Here is what he said:

> Slavery was the technological underpinning of high civilization and of history until very recent times. Slavery was abolished only when the biological energy of man was displaced by mechanical energy in the industrial revolution.
>
> What about the role of ethics in this story of man's inhumanity to man? Slavery is condemned in the Old Testament only when the chroniclers are concerned with the Egyptian captivity. There is no condemnation of slavery in the centers of Jewish culture in Palestine; there is no suggestion of the

> immorality of this peculiar institution. In the New Testament, Christ assures us that the poor will always be with us. In Plato's view, some men were natural slaves. His opinion was echoed by no less a figure in our own history than Thomas Jefferson. *Slavery became immoral when it became technologically obsolete.*

While I certainly would not claim that technological solutions can he found to all human, national and international problems, believe that the categorical statement that such solutions are absolutely impossible has in it a fair-sized element of error. Educational technology must never be used, to condition young people to live in a world of standardization, conformity and alienation.

Educational media are crucial to the individual learner because they represent an alternative means of his accessing relevant information in the absence of a traditional teacher/lecturer. In the general sense, educational media include texts, workbooks, programmed books and other print materials; tapes, records and other audio materials: filmstrips, motion pictures, study prints and other photographic materials; games, realia, apparatus and a number of other materials; charts, signs, maps, and other graphic materials; dioramas, bulletin boards, felt boards and other displays; as well as a variety of other cue-organizing resources which serve as the carriers of messages. Many of these media-based messages are accessed by the individual learner in his classroom, others are obtained in a school resource center, and still others must be obtained from remote locations. Television, dial access systems, shared-time computers, and the telephone are all techniques for accessing remote educational material.

It is not necessary to have sophisticated technology in order to individualize learning and many "audiovisual" resources currently in use are quite well suited to this application. Finally, recognizing, that the term technology refers as much to a process as to a set of hardware and media alternatives, it is useful to examine how the process of technology may alter the man-machine relationship in the days and years to come. John W. Loughary forecasts the ways in a systematic application of technology could greatly improve our educational capabilities. The focus of his reasoning suggests the use of information-processing technologies to develop a school data base comprised of curriculum files and student-descriptive files. Then, through the analysis of school management needs, evaluative research needs, and instructional needs it should be possible to reallocate those functions which technology can appropriately perform, freeing professional educators to provide more personalized attention to individual students.

Appointment of a national Commission on Instructional Technology under the Public Broadcasting Act points up the need for broad participation in defining agreeable boundaries of the field, locating the problem within its human, social, and institutional contexts, and considering priorities of emphasis and action. The Commission's assignment is complicated by a posture of pessimism in a new power structure of instructional technology, or "learning systems," particularly among those involved in adapting computers to instruction. This posture appears to be based on the partial truth that instructional technological devices have failed to live up to overstated performance promises when adopted by the schools. Consequently, all technological innovation, including those in various stages of R&D., are viewed as vulnerable to the dreadful disclosure of fraud when submitted to the pragmatic test of trial and adoption in actual instructional situations. The fact that many schools and colleges are virtually without funds intensifies the new pessimism toward instructional technology.

Underlying this pessimism or defeatism are several identifiable factors which lie deep in the educational system as sources of many problems of instruction. The salience of these factors is well known to those who have (a) participated directly in technological innovation in public school systems, colleges, and mass military training; (b) done both contextual and evaluation research on what hitherto have been known as 'new media in education: and (c) tried to develop viable theories dealing with the new media in instruction." Among these factors are the following:

1. An overexpectation of effects from any given gadget or process, simple or complex, adapted to instruction from some other area, such as entertainment (motion pictures, television) and automated industrial processes and commercial transactions (computers).
2. Measurement of effects" (evaluation) of the "new media" by instruments and techniques which are non-metric in the mathematical sense of measurement and insensitive to dimensions of human response that may be of much greater importance than the "behavioral objectives" they are designed to "measure."
3. A "scientific" outlook among learning theorists, instructional systems analysts and designers, programmed instruction developers, etc., which (a) ignores the importance and operation of intuition in classroom interaction, and (b) prescribes narrow behavioral objectives and their criterial "measures.".
4. An inertial property of educational and adjunct institutions which makes them resistant to change, slow to innovate, and methodologically non-adaptive when innovation is tried..

5. An irrelevance of much of learning theory of classroom teaching situations as they exist in reality, rather than in psychology laboratories.

6. A curriculum which is frequently misphased, overintellectualized, and irrelevant to the individual needs and social milieu of large numbers of students, and consequently operative at best among bright and/or docile students responsive to pressures for compliance from both parents and teachers.

7. An overextended period of compulsory or socially prescribed education which induces boredom and maintains the status quo in a seller's market in formal education, and an underdeveloped program of continuing education which is particularly receptive and adaptive to instructional technology.

8. A narrow exclusiveness in the Educational Establishment, including the U.S. Office of Education and professional educational organizations, which equates education and instruction with public school systems and colleges, and ignores the educational and training programs of business, industry, the military services, etc.

A concept of instructional technology

It seems the better part of valor in the present state of things to adopt a moderate view of the scope of *instructional* technology. Otherwise, we will become involved in a range of concerns from team teaching to underground, windowless schools. Essentially, instructional technology in its modem usage, involves the *management* of ideas, procedures, money, machines, and people in the instructional process. As such, it, involves:

1. A physical device(s) which mediates information transmission,

2. A system of instruction of which this device(s) is one of several components; and
3. A range of mediating options involving progression in (a) requirements for physical alteration of the "classroom", (b) remoteness in time and space between the tutor-planner and the student, (c) sophistication of design of programmed information exchange between "tutor" and student; (d) complexity and cost of hardware; (e) level of technical skills required for equipment construction, installation, "debugging," operation, and maintenance; M independence from classroom teacher control or continuous monitoring in the operation of the device centered "teaching"; (g) additional manpower required by way of paraprofessional personnel for use of the instructional technology, and (h) role changes and new skills required of "classroom" teachers in (1) management of the technology, and (2) other and/or new non-structured, non-mediated teaching activities essential to personality development, humanistic growth, and cultivation of values, all of which lie outside the present and foreseeable potential of instructional technology as herein considered.

While the progression in technological devices indicated above is not deliberately sequenced in order of increasing administrator and teacher resistance to technological innovations in education, such a heuristic resistance sequence is implicit.

Classroom teacher ritual

The current and historical role of the classroom teacher is highly ritualized. Any major change in ritual is likely to be resisted as an invasion of the sanctuary by the barbarians. Ritualization in teaching is flexible enough to permit idiosyncrasies of personal style, arrangement of the daily schedule, police methods, pacing, etc., but major characteristics of ritual tend to be invariant.

Two of these invariants are (1) teacher control of the teaching-testing-grading-reward-punishment processes, and (2) face-to-face, interaction with students.

These two variants in rituals of teaching are likely to be important determinants in ' the trial and adoption of technological innovation and in its effectiveness in either event at the classroom level. *Any sudden or substantial reduction* of dominance status and/or domain of activities of the classroom teacher, any major change in the interpersonal teacher-student communication situation, or any systematic attempt to scientize and rationalize the intuitively determined 'interaction patterns of the teacher is likely to elicit at least some teacher hostility and resistance.

The attitude of the cllassroom teacher toward any instructional innovation—technological or otherwise is of paramount importance While trial or adoption of innovation may be formalized at the federal, state, or community levels of control, it is in the individual school and individual classroom that the transaction occurs functionally.

Indeed, it may be that the more or less generally accepted theory of instructional innovation as (a) originating from the outside, and (b) proceeding from the top down in the hierarchical structure, carries within it the seeds of its own failures or imperfections by omitting participation of classroom teachers in adaption and adoption decisions at the local policy making and implementation level. Some remarkable research findings with direct bearing on the effects of teacher attitudes on student behavior are currently being spelled out by Robert Rosenthal and his associates using the concept of communication of expectancy.

In studies of the introduction of programmed instruction in Denver, Colorado, it was reported that students performed better under teachers favorable to programmed instruction even when the sole function of the teacher was to maintain order. Put another way, better results were obtained from students Under Programmed instruction when the expectancy of teachers was in a favorable direction, and this expectance effect occurred independently of the participational activity role of the teachers in the instructional process.

Apparently, human beings are highly sensitive to both intended and unintended expectancy curing behavior of other human beings in dominant roles. Rosenthal reports that in an experiment on perception of people through photographs, subjects were asked to rate the experimenters an the "honesty" variable. This variable could be operative only after the experiment, and could occur in tabulating and summing, the results. Errors in tabulation could be random or in the direction of confirming the hypothesis held by the experimenter, and tabulation and computational errors could be large or small.

Both tabulation and computational errors occurred. Among those who erred in the direction of the expectancy of their hypotheses, tabulation errors were larger. Mean ratings on an honesty scale by the experimental subjects were significantly lower for those experimenters who made errors in the direction of their hypothesis, i.e., experimenter expectancy. This suggests that subjects in the experiment were able to detect some cues in the behavior of experimenters which predicted beyond chance the subsequent errors in experimental data processing.

This apparent sensitivity of subjects to unintentional and perhaps non-formally coded cues to expectancy of results manifested by authority figures in an authority-structured social situation can be related to teacher influence on student performance in the direction of their expectancy hypothesis in the Denver trials of programmed instruction—especially when monitoring teachers exercised only the police function of preserving order in the classroom.

Even more remarkable results of teacher expectance on student development of competencies are reported by Robert Rosenthal and Lenore Jacobson in their recent books Pygmalion in the Classroom. Teachers in a San Francisco Bay Area school were told that about 20 percent of the students in each class included in the experiment had been identified through extensive testing as having unusual potential for intellectual gains. No such extensive testing had been done. The names of the 20 percent identified as having this unusual potential were selected randomly. In this experiment no special programs, tutoring activities, or enrichment activities were involved. The only new element was that of favorable teacher expectation—teacher attitude toward the "unusual" pupils—and presumably consequent verbal and nonverbal expression by the teachers of this attitude toward these students.

To oversimplify interesting results, "unusual' students made significantly greater gains in IQ than the non-unusuals. The implications of these findings are difficult to overestimate. They suggest that (a) teacher expectancy, often operating at the unintentional level, is a variable of major importance in the instructional and developmental processes; and (b) students are highly sensitive and responsive to teacher expectancy along previously unsuspected dimensions of perception and growth.

It is reasonable to assume teacher expectance

operates negatively as well as positively, as suggested by the Denver findings. That is, negative teacher expectancy may have a depressing, or leveling, or inhibiting, " hostility-arousing effect on student development Yet, as far as, teacher selection and certification procedures do not ordinarily include the criterion of the true believer in the "unusual' growth potential of students. It may be hypothesized that all innovators and agents of change tend to be what Eric Hoffer calls "true believers," oriented toward a better future of mankind, an improvement of the human condition of everyone; and that one of the most important aspects of instructional technology is the inherent expectancy of educational improvement shared by its advocates. The corollary is that instructional technology fails or disappoints when its implementation falls into the hands of skeptics and infidels whose habituated classroom rituals have attained doctrinal significance, and consequently whose expectancy of ritualistic change is negative.

To crystallize the argument, it should be borne in mind that:

1. Many of the troublesome problems of instructional technology are essentially further manifestations of the troublesome problems and properties of instruction in the American educational system.
2. The fashionable attitude of pessimism and "poohpooh" toward instructional technology is particularly evident among an elite of the supra, Educational Establishment for whom the world of instructional technology originated last year or the year before and consist largely of promised but undelivered computer regulation of the process of individualized, multi-tracked instructional programs, task assignments, and performance monitoring.
3. At least some, if not many, of the significant

variables of in-school growt h and development of students lie beyond the cognizance of learning theory, and the consequences of these variables escape the narrowly prescribed "first order," behaviorally operationalized objectives of instruction and their criterial "measures" The process of innovation has been studied on the normative rather than the explanatory, i.e., theoretical, level and consequently the literature on innovation provides few cues for acceleration and adoption of desirable changes in the system of instruction.

4. The classroom teacher is by training and institutional control a prisoner of the orthodox ritualization of the educational system, negatively disposed to automation, and perhaps less effective as a gatekeeper than as a positive or negative expectancy reflector.

It follows that substantial, difficult, and not-clearly-defined changes must be made in the educational system both for its own effective survival and in order to accelerate the rate of development, adoption, and optimum use of instructional technology, assuming that instructional technology can be justified in the first place.

Justification of instructional technology

Instructional technology is more justified by its own logic than by empirical studies of its effectiveness in facilitating "learning. Empirical studies often ignore critical variables, and typically "measure only those results which are easiest to operationalize within the state of the art of criterial specification and educational testing. The notion of "unobtrusive measures" has scarcely penetrated educational research, and at least some of the vigorously Promoted techniques of multivariate analysis are too often used as substitutes for thinking. This is not to say that empirical research has no place in uncovering important relationships or evaluating procedures and progress in instruction, but only that too often it is overburdened by techniques and designed with impoverished insight and imagination.

The development, use, and improvement of instructional technology, as defined in this article, is justified in general by the fact that American schools operate as a formative institution of a highly technological society and should therefore incorporate, as appropriate, this characteristic of the larger society as well as other idealized values. In a sense, this principle of justification is aesthetic and can rest at that without decisive challenge.

However, since aesthetics generates much subjectivity and little objectivity, stimulates lofty dialogue at the philosophical level and restless, insistent controversy in relation to specific events, it is desirable to get down to tangible criteria in justifying instructional technology.

It may be said reflectively that instructional technology is justified if and when it:

(a) makes available a mode or multimodes of representation on any of several levels of reality, without constrains of geography or of real time, and hitherto not available for instruction

(b) provides a model of behavior otherwise unavailable, in scarce supply, or lacking authenticity or correctness of definition, and preferably when it provides opportunity for the student to compare his imitative behavior with that of the model.

(c) sequences and, within reasonable limits and without undue restraints, manages stimulus inputs and response outputs on a desirable individualized and structured basis otherwise difficult or impossible to achieve;

(d) stores, retrieves, and rapidly processes a large amount of important and useful information not otherwise readily available, or, if available, too time-consuming to process manually.

(e) involves desirable latent functions of a critical nature in the instructional process or system which, because they are not immediately related to improved and measured student progress, may escape proper assessment or even official observation.

None of these five criteria in necessarily independent of the other four. All can be combined in instructional systems involving simple or complex hardware, or electronic components. Also, it goes without saying that this brief list of criteria is not intended to be either definitive or exhaustive.

Minimizing contingencies of instructional technology

For what it is worth, it may be said reflectively, and with some empirical evidence, that the effectiveness of instructional technology will be less than optimum 'if and when it:

(a) incorporates the format of other modes of instruction known to be relatively inefficient and ineffective instructionally, i.e, when McLuhan's "rearview mirror' effect occurs;

(b) fails to challenge or slows down the natural pace of progression of students and thus induces student boredom and/or resentment;

(c) rapidly reaches a point of diminishing returns and thus bernmes monotonous and unrewarding;

(d) severely and continuously reduces the social process of education i.e., face-to-face interpersonal interactions, group participation, etc.;

(e) requires logistical beyond the capacity of the system to provide in proper time-phase and matching characteristics, and without heavy encumbrance of hardware, additional personnel, or hard-to-find dollars.

Priorities and emphases

It may be reasonably expected that all of us will sooner or later come to some decisions on priorities. A set of questions such as the following deserve consideration and allocation of priorities:.

1 Should motion pictures, filmstrips, radio, and other media, currently not considered as technological innovations but as adoptions, be taken for granted, or should they be re-examined, for; currency of content, state of the art such as employment of more involving and perhaps less isomorphic symbolism, extent of adoption, logistical adequacy, etc.?

Should emphasis now placed on the newer technologies, such as ITV and PTV, individually prescribed instruction, computer regulated instruction, etc., be intensified, or should they undergo more extensive feasibility, operational suitability, and effectiveness testing, bearing in mind the kinds of variables already discussed, and the present limitations and necessary modifications of research procedures and techniques?

2 Should efforts to diffuse instructional technology and increase its effectiveness be time-phased from the elementary school, which is more open to innovation, and progressively to the high school and college which are more conservative and less open to changes in teacher role and ritual?

Should the efforts to diffuse instructional technology and increases its effectiveness be more emphasized among formally certified "systems" of education, such as public schools and colleges, which often defy systems analysis simply because they are systematically chaotic, or should they be more emphasized on the para-formal educational institutions of industry, commerce, and the military services which are better systematized and more definitively goal oriented ?.

3 Within the formally structured and certified educational "systems", should emphasis on the employment of instructional technology be directed to use among those schools serving the "culturally deprived" student population, or should it be directed to use among those schools serving the family reinforced, docile, compliant and thus more "teachable" student population ?

Again within the formally structured and certified educational "systems", should emphasis on instructional technology be placed on the full-time student population, or on the continuing education population among whom the struggle is greater, the need more acute, and the motivation possibly more intense?.

4. What changes are required in teaching rituals and functions in order to increase allocations of time to learning activities of students directly related to 'new media," and in teachers' expectancy images of students so they are perceived as human beings with primordial capacities to learn, "turn on," and develop on higher levels?.

What balances and directions are required in the development of the newer more complex technologies of instruction and/or their employment, for both the essential individualizing and the essential socializing processes of education?

The list of questions is not exhaustive, and their formulation does not exclude the middle ground from consideration. Omitted from the list are questions dealing with the important issues of teacher education, strategies of innovation, and research methodologies. Also omitted are questions of use of technology in public relations, class scheduling, library controls, etc., not because they are unimportant but because they attenuate the problems of instructional technology. However, we will all be in error if we ignore these areas of application.

The system approach

Throughout the above discussion, the systems concept is embedded in various points. Like cost effectiveness, operations research, the cognitive and affective domains, and other terms on current display in the best company, the systems concept is being scourged mercilessly in educational discourse; nevertheless it is imperative that instructional technology be approached within a central concept of instruction as a system, and not as the installation of appliances, or the design of school buildings in the round. A system is no more or no less than an arrangement in which everything is related to everything else so that the malfunctioning of any part affects the system output or outcome.

The systems concept is not fully explicated or articulated in its educational applications and implications but its seminal ideas are clear and simple and need not await the master blueprint to be accepted and acted upon. Perhaps those neat, big or little flow charts with boxes, circles, and arrows that appear so elegantly professional and slightly awesome in the new educational literature are a necessary and useful step in beginning to take a fresh look at instructional technology.

6

General Aspects of Educational Technology

The first industrial revolution was the product of various intentions which the instructor had made on the other hand the second industrial resolution is the product of the scientists and technicians. It is thought that the atomic power, rochet engines and automation are in fact in their technological childhood. In this chapter the impact of automation on education as a practice has been studied in general. Of all of the phenomena which have resulted from the application of science to industrial and military problems, automation is, or should be, of greatest interest to the professional educator. The problems and promises inherent in automation are directly related to education. Educators must re-examine science and technology in the second half of the 20th century. What are needed in 1957 and for many years to come are (a) a through assessment of the nature of the new technological world and its implications for education; (b) a revision of educational organization, procedures and content, which will close the gap between the rocket-like progress of technology and the snail's pace of education; and (c) the application of useful concepts and processes from the new technology to the educational enterprise itself in order to close this ever-widening gap.

Such a procedure will be a serious and difficult matter. It is not here suggested that educcators take up a new fad. If automation and its related concepts are grasped by eager curriculum workers, school administrators, and professors in teaching educational institutions, at the level of understanding and Performance that some of the recent fads in education have been handled, we shall be worse off than before. We emerged from the "group dynamics" fad witnessing hundreds of People at various levels in education talking about a process they didn't understand and fooled by their acquisition of the vocabulary, attempting to do things with group processes and with the results of group dynamics research that couldn't be done as well as not doing other important things that should have been done. We are still gripped today by a "three Rs" and a "gifted" fad which, presumably will be dropped at the introduction of some other new idea that will make "experts" of its first practitioners long before they nave an inkling of what they are either doing or talking about. Automation cannot be treated this way. To repeat, it is a serious and difficult business and offers no haven for the educator looking for something with which to impress the Teachers' Institute next fall.

In as much as the audiovisual approach to communication is, strictly speaking, an attempt to solve a difficult human problem with technology, and in as much as ideas have recently been advanced in several quarters that audiovisual technology might become automate, it follows that students of audiovisual communication must lead in the examination of the relationships of automation and education. The writer proposes to do this under three general headings, this paper covering the first. The three headings are:

1. General Aspects
2. Automatizing the Classroom.
3. Built-In Dangers

In considering the topic of automation and education from the audiovisual point of view, there is a temptation to go directly the central question continually raised by Dr. Eurich, namely: Can we, with audiovisual materials and devices such as film or TV, extend the range of the master teacher? However, because of the complex nature of the automation concept and because it will have other effects on education which, in turn, will affect the audiovisual movement, ;it is necessary to begin the study by analyzing the more general relationships of automation with education. This background study is the theme of this article.

The idea that the Second Industrial Revolution and automation, one of its main products will have a profound on is not exactly new. Statements abound to this effect, including one of the author's. However, the existence of ideas and their immediate or even consequent effect on educational practice is very difficult to establish, fads excepted There is, as well known generally though to be a 50-year lag between idea and practice. With the speed of the new technology, symbolized by the space statellite this 50-year wait simply cannot be tolerated. We are living in an era of fantastic change and everyone in education, from the superintendent to the janitor, must recognize this fact and be prepared to act upon it. Dean Irving R. Melbo, in addressing a conference of school administrators, cited a need at the administrative level for educational statesmen. He then went on to define the characteristics, of such a statesman, including the ability to recognize issues. In speaking to this point, he emphasized this modern problem of change in education:

The ability to recognize issues is all too often lacking among our educational administrators. But perhaps the fault lies with the institutions which trained them, because no man can recognize issues if he has not learned to think in terms of issues. The simple truth is that great economic and social forces flow with a tidal sweep over communities that are only half conscious of that which is befalling them. Wise statesmen are those who foresee what time is thus bringing and endeavor to shape institutions and to mold men's thought and purpose in accordance with the change that is silently surrounding them.

And, as the Second Industrial Revolution with its automatic control so sweeps silently into our communities, all schoolmen would do well to remember the words of Whitehead, written over 20 years ago:

Our sociological theories, our political philosophy, our practical maxims of business our political economy, and our doctrines of education, are derived from an unbroken tradition of great thinkers and of practical examples from the age of Plato to the end of the last century. The whole of this tradition is warped by the vicious assumption that each 'generation will substantially live amid the conditions governing the lives of its fathers and will transmit those conditions to mould with equal force the lives of its children. We are living in the first period of human history for which this assumption is false.

Automation is one of the reasons why the immediate future will bring conditions that cannot be accounted for in the experience of mankind. Automation will radically alter our system of education. It will be well, if we are to recognize and study these issues to attempt to define this phenomenon.

Automation is one of those concepts capable of several definitions. This is no doubt due to the fact that its meaning has not yet been fully developed. At present automation is a term better described than precisely defined; automation represents a territory that can be mapped but not surveyed to the decimal point. Drucker, in his very illuminating discussion states that, "Automation can be defined simply though superficially as the use of machines to run machines".

Macmillan indicates the range of meaning inherent the term, He speaks of.

> .... a great ententsion in the use of automatic devices to take over the simpler kinds of work previously done by the men in charge of machines. The word "automation" has been applied to this process and widely adopted. It was first used several years ago by engineers of the Ford Motor Company in the United States to describe their methods for automatically conveying workpieces between successive machines; but since then it has come to have a much wider significance implying any process in which the lower functions of human operator-both physical and mental are taken over by self-acting devices. Interpreted in this way, the word "automation" clearly means more than mere mechanization ....

The CIO Committee of Economic Policy refers to a three-level description developed by Baldwin and Shultz of M.I.T. They are:

1. The level of integration or "Detroit automation," which means the linking together of conventional machines so that the work proceeds from one to the other without human intervention.
2. The level of "feedback" control, which means the introduction of computing machines into the system. The computing machines record and store information make computations and feed the results back into the system establishing complete control of the whole operation.

Examples of automation

As will be shown later the descriptions above represent

only the hard-core mechanical attributes of automation and indicate that *the* concept as it is developing today has abstract ideational properties which may be even more important. However, these abstract properties are not possible without the solid grounding in industrial and scientific developments. To increase understanding, then of the basis for these descriptive definitions, some of the examples of automatic production may be helpful.

The following examples, for the most part are taken form the CIO report. Others could be cited. The Cleveland plant tuning out Ford engines under the "Detroit automation" system links a battery of machines on a line 1,500 feet long with automatic machine tools performing over 500 operations. The plant processes 154 engine blocks on hour with 41 workers. The same operation under older mass-producing methods would take 117 workers.

The Wall Street Journal is the authority for the statement that Raytheon's television and radio division plant will be able to turn out 1,000 radios in a day with only two workers on the line as compared with a former need of 200 workers. Office automation is shown in the John Plain mail order house in Chicago, where a computer handles 90,000 tallies a day in keeping track of an 8,000 item catalog. Insurance companies now going to computer operation are represented by one cited which makes 7,000 daily billings, 20,000 monthly calculations for dividends and 130,000 calculations for agency commissions at a saving of from 175 to 225 clerical personnel. Finally it is reported that, General Mills had produced an automatic machine which will produce electronic equipment. This machine, it is claimed, will require only two workers and a supervisor and has a capacity of over 200,000 assemblies a month.

While these are examples of automation in office

and factory, it should be emphasized that they are, as yet examples. Outside of modem oil refineries which are almost fully automatic there are practically no fully automatic plants yet in operation. As John I. Snyder Jr., president of U.S. Industries points out, many industries are coming closer to it and have already automatized one or more parts of the production process. His own U.S. Industries was in 1955, operating only the fully automatic factory a government-owned, 155mm shell plant in Rockford, Illinois. However, a recent study by the Research Institute of America of 1,000 major companies found that 16 per-cent saw automation of a factor in their industry at the present time and that no additional 23 percent predicted extensive automation in their industry within a decade. Only one-third of the respondents felt that automation would never affect them.

Characterisation of automation

When automatic operations of various kinds are looked at together certain characteristics seem to emerge. These characteristics are not mechanical or technical in a machine sense. Rather they are conceptual and as such have educational significance. The first and probably the most important characteristic of the new industrial revolution is the concept of systems.

While this concept has discussed before in connection with audiovisual administration, its pervasiveness in business and industry any large-scale organization has yet to be realized. The systems idea is best grasped in connection with an offices which is undergoing automation. While many process-billing posting, etc.—will be done by automatic machinery in such a setup, the important element, are the planning necessary for the whole procedure, the location and function of necessary personnel, the types of forms used, etc. A system has to be created which gears all of these elements into a smooth flow with controls feeding back information throughout the process. The system is much more important than the computer which calculates interest rates, for example. A representative of a firm which installs automatic processing in office was heard to remark recently that it would take his firm eight years to install a system in a large company.

The problem of systems and systems-analysis is complex and cannot be treated here at any length. Much automatic machinery can do certain routine work infinitely better and faster than man. Aircraft warning devices are an example of this. But somewhere in any operation, there must be men. Men, machines and information have all to be coordinated into a system which may begin when a prospect is furnished an insurance salesman or a blip appears upon a radarscope and ends with the widow receiving a check or the refueling of an interceptor plane after its mission has been accomplished. No longer can the in between operations be considered piecemeal. Automation means system intograted with system.

Secondly, such systems and such potentials for rapid production need control. The old fairy story of the salt-making machine that went on and on grinding salt could easily be translated into a modern engineer's nightmare. There are many elements here and at different levels. At the level of the mechanics of the production line, information is needed constantly as to the condition of the machines and the work and at the marketing level, information is needed as to style, inventory price, etc. If a machine gets too hot, information must come back to a control point and orders issued for lubrication, reduction of speed or some other remedies if too many of the wrong color widgets are popping off the end of the line, information again must go to a control point so that fewer pink widgets and more blue ones are produced.

The constant here and a general characteristic of automatic operation is the flow of information and the control of the system by that information.

The third general characteristic of automation springs logically from the two which precede it. The systems and control characteristics of automation demand thorough analysis and long-range planning. The huge capital involved for example, in automatizing an operation means that the operation cannot be carried on by caprice. Once an automatic operation is underway, it is very costly tostop it for extensive changes. Hence, accurate planning is required. This planning is obviously one of the main factors in the eight-year installation problem described above in connection with another insurance firm.

The planning, however cannot proceed without analysis. Neither can a system function indefinitely without analysis. This is the reason that the terms "operations analysis" or "operational research' are closely allied to the development of automation, and for that matter of all modem technology. The term "operational research" is usually used to refer to the study of management problems from the point of view of the mathematician, the physical scientist, and the biological scientist. The operational research staff, for example, in a military headquarters attempts to strip a problem down to its bare essentials create a mathematical model of it and solve for the best answer. As Dr. John Abrams of the Royal Canadian Air Force pointed out in military operational research use is made of such things a probability statistics, the theory of games, search problems, and the newer theories of value and decision. These of course are all in the realm of mathematics. Methodologies from other sciences are also used.

While there is no doubt that the armed forces of

several countries have pioneered in the area of operational research, the term is now being heard in reference to similar problems in industry. The very existence of computers as part of the automation process makes possible the solution of complex mathematical problems relating to operational research in a very short time.

The mention of decision making in connection with automation highlights the fourth characteristic of the process which is decision making. Drucker points out that, in order to control such processes and systems and to make and carry out the necessary plans many more better educated managers will be needed in the future . Decisions dealing with a complex system will have complex consequences. The implications here for education are tremendous.

Finally, although it should be obvious that, it should be necessary to point out that automation and its clusters of systems is a high-order product of technology. That, it is a highly technical business. While the operations themselves may be reduced to watching an occasional gauge or checking the accuracy of a bill for an insurance premium that has just come through a machine, the machines themselves and the systems within which they operate are exceedingly complex Maintenance, for example, will require very able technicians. The engineering behind some of the equipment involved in automation also presents great problems of design.

Then these, are some of the characteristics of automation and its associated processes and systems: (a) the concept of systems, W, the flow and control of information, (c) scientific analysis and long-range planning, (d) an increase in the need for wise decision making and (e) a high-level technology.

Those who sense that all social economic forces affect education in general as well as specific ways will realize that a list of the effects of automation on education could be almost endless. Obviously, there are concerns about technological unemployment, even if it may be temporary and the age structure of our population for the next 20 years will bring less people into the labor force than we need. The need for maximum productivity for prosperity placed against a reduction in the labor force will hurry, rather than stay the development of automation. A shorter work week seems to be inevitable. Industry will be interested as never before in a predictable expanding stable market the risks are too great in capital, etc. to break down an automated system. This would imply that industry may have a stake in some kind of an annual wage. The initial high costs of capitalization for completely automatic production may operate to farther change our economy in the direction of more much business. One authority has suggested that, with a great sameness of product possible from automatic factories, the day of the artisan and hand-worker may once again bloom.

All of these and many more possible social economic effects have educational implications. It is too early to say what many of them will actually turn out to be However, there are a number of more direct effects that can be identified and these effects will be pronounced at all levels of education. Consider carefully the following quotations.

Automation's most important impact will not be on employment but on the qualifications and functions of employees. And this increase both in the numbers of managers and in the demands made on them may well be the largest of all the social impacts of Automation.

One large manufacturing company figures that it

will need seven thousand college graduates in a year, once it is automated, just to keep going, today it hires three hundred annually. But the need is above all qualitative for better educated people. The "trained barbarian, ' the man who has acquired high gadgeteering skill, will not do. Even in routine jobs, Automation will require ability to think a trained imagination and good judgment plus some skill in logical methods, some mathematical understanding and some ability well above the elementary level to read and write in a word, the normal equipment of educated people. Under Automation, a school could do a student no greater disservice than to prepare him, as so many do today, for his first Job. If there is one thing certain under Automation, it is that the job-even the bottom job-will change radically and often.

In the conditions of modern life, the rule is absolute. The race which does not value trained intelligence is doomed. Not all your heroism, or all your social charm neither all your wit or all your victories at land or at sea, can move back the finger of fate. Today we maintain ourselves. Tomorrow science will have moved forward yet one more step, and there will be no appeal from the judgment which will then be pronounced on the uneducated.

Information theory is the science underlying all exchange of information and is of especial importance in the development of telecommunications and automatic control systems. The treatment adopted by the author has enabled him to give a clear account of recent developments without requiring knowledge of mathematics in excess of that which may reasonably be exprected from the professional engineer or physicist.

The First Industrial Revolution, the revolution of the "dark satanic mills" was the devaluation of the human arm by the competition of machinery. There is no rate of pay at which a United States pick-and-shovel laborer can live which is low enough to compete with the work of a steam shovel as an excavator, The modem industrial revolution is similarly bound to devalue the human brain, at least in its simpler and more routine decisions. Of course, just as the skilled carpenter, the skilled mechanic, the skilled dressmaker have in some degree survived the First Industrial Revolution, so the skilled scientist and the skilled administrator may survive the second. However, taking the Second Revolution as accomplished, the average human being of mediocre attainments or less has nothing to sell that is worth anyone's money to buy.

These quotations are enough to give any thoughtful educator pause. Some of their possible implications and the implications in general of automation may be discussed under four headings:

1. The curriculum and program of studies.
2. Administration.
3. The possibilities in automatizing the process of education itself.
4. Changes required delineated.

The first problem under the program of studies category is the role and the placement of subject matter. It can be suggested that those educators who relegate "subject matter' to limbo or who suggest that 'we are only work through subject matter to something else" are echoing the cliche's of the 1920s without meaning in 1957. For certain groups of students, subject matter per se will have a new importance. This is not to suggest that all the gains in dealing with individual persons, in attempting to change behavior through problem solving, etc. need be thrown out. Does it suggest that a technological society needs technical information in the possession of a large group of its members. Specifically, mathematics will continue to play a greater role than ever in our lives. Thorough a revision of the classical mathematics curriculum at the secondary level is called for, in addition to a strengthening of the Program at the elementary level solid geometry, for example, is according to many modern mathemeticians, an interesting but absolute subject and should be dropped. The high school mathematics program can be revised so that, for example, the elements of calculus will be taught to some students in high school.

The science phases of the elementary curriculum need revision and strengthening in many elementary school in the United State, science instruction is a joke. If so, this may be a pretty high price for our society to pay for a few laughs. Actually, at least for some children, the self-contained classroom in the upper-elementary level with its extreme emphasis on :social living should be due for a thorough going over. It may be that for some children, we will want some form of departmentalization with a pushing downward of some of the elements of the present high school curriculum. This will mean an earlier transition from a developmental curriculum than most of the people in elementary education are now willing to make.

Another concept that must be re-examined and at the very highest levels of education is the concept of general education. The last 20 years have brought great pressures for general education for an education so that we may appreciate our common heritage, etc. Survey courses, Great Books, the Harvard essentials, exploration courses, and work-experierce programs are all examples of this sort. There has been a great deal more worry among the Mark Van Dorens, Mortimer Adlers and A. Whitney Griswolds about whether or not cur technicians, engineers and scientists could talk to each other than whether or not they were good technicians, engineers or scientists. The spokesmen for general education have actually attempted to create a specialist in general education under the guise of dealing with the well-known ignorance of specialists.

It is a moot point whether or not a highly technical society can survive and maintain itself without highly specialized technological know-how. It takes time to acquire his know-how. Without decrying general education, it would seem that this extreme emphasis upon it should be re-examined with a view to reducing the time devoted to it. It is recognized that this is in opposition to Drucker's position that the managerial talent of the future will have to have a general education. It is my feeling that Mr. Drucker has become enmeshed in his own net in this instance. Management is, or will become, a highly skilled profession. Mr. Drucker does not want general education he wants general professional education and the distinction is important.

The implication of a few paragraphs above—that not all students should have the some education—can be stated in the proposition that education for an age of automation will require homogeneous grouping of students in the public schools and recognition of different patterns of preparation.

The well-known facts of psychology relating to the extreme variations in individuals and the fact that individuals may be homogeneous in one respect and not in others will require a re-examination of even the principle of homogeneous grouping. But it is still reasonable to expect that not all high school students will be able or find it necessary to take the elements calculus The great problem here is to find ways and means of shortening and improving the general education periods so that all students can function as citizens, parents, etc., and at the same time, meet the demands of a technological society for specialists. Perhaps the greatest educational dilemma of our time may be stated as follows: if these two objectives come into complete conflict, a technological society, in order to survive, has no choice but to pick technology. We may not like the world we so create, but we must recognize it for what it is.

Computers, cyclotrons and magnetrons—all paraphernalia of the age automation-point up another great fact that is powerful eough to shake the structure of the whole curriculum from the kindergarten to the graduate school. This a problem which most curriculum people have ignored by the simple process of ducking their heads in the sand of "attitude formation" and "problem-solving skills." Incidentaly, it has also been completely ignored by their opposite members of the Saturday Review set who still think that Aristotle had no need to count the number of teeth in his wife's mouth. The poets, the Greek plays, the scciodrarna and he resour unit do not necessarily have the answer to this problem. The solution must lie in thorough revision of content and the development of means to teach more to more people in less time.

The systems concept, and related matters emphasize the fact that, while group dynamics has not yet got beyond the stage of a primitive religion in most curriculum circles, it has the key to many problems that will beset an automatized world. Human relations, group relations, even international relations become proper subjects of study and necessary areas in which to develop real skill and proper attitudes. Again, here the problem may be methodological. The solution will not be found in the technique used by a professor of education in holding a "buzz session" or in having committee reports made in class—any more than it will be found in some of the so-called "workshops" run by school districts under the euphemism of an in-service training program. We need to develop content and method which yield measurable results in this field.

There are many other implications for a curriculum content in an age of automation. To create decision makers means that the thought processes of student must have experienced conflicts and made decisions; to analyze, to plan, to create systems and to take the long-range view to be creative. Those information-mongers, those fact-purveyors who felt that the position stated above with regard to subject matter was their meat had better keep this fundamental in mind. No mountain of facts will do more than provide the background for this process. Our new curriculum must do so, but not in any sloppy way, based on the assumption that if the children learn how to solve the problem of waste paper in the cafeteria over a semester's period of time, they have demonstrated outstanding ability in a pattern thinking.

The problems of additional leisure time, the problems of vocational training in a world where a vocations will change and buttons or magnetic tapes take their place all need consideration for the new curriculum. The best that we can say is that we have had curriculum challenges before, but never of the intensity and urgency that the coming age of automation presents us.

The second category of possible effects is that of administration. The new management concepts-systems, operational research, the use of the theory of games, etc.—all have much to offer school administrators. The theory of school administration—in my opinion already somewhat creaky-needs a thorough re-examination in the light of these new developments. It is not overstating the case to that education for an age of automation needs an administrative theory that is at least able to keep up with it. This is a great challenge to theorists in the field of administration and to practicing administrators. If administrators are to lead, it would be well to begin by streamlining their own operations to fit the demands of a new world. Third, much need to be done in considering how far we may go in automatizing the process of educations itself. Here, as was mentioned before, lies the direct relationship between the audiovisual field and the concepts of automation. This topic will be the subject of the second of these studies. Can the somewhat cold process of closed-circuit television, for example, increase educational efficiency without losing something in the process?.

Finally, when all this is added up, what, changes can be expected in our intellectual structure-in the context of education" itself? Certain things have been mentioned—a re-examination of curriculum theory, especially as it applies to the program of studies and of administrative theory. It is to be expected that new bodies of such theory will be created and studies conducted on hypotheses based upon these theories.

Actually education, as a subject of study, has stood on a plateau for about 20 years. The audiovisual field is one exception to this statement. The curriculum books still say much the same thing, the speakers at institutes and meetings are still reworking the old material. Education, as a discipline, is in the position it was around 1900 when a new graduate content was created almost overnight by Thorndike, Dewey, Monroe and a few others.

We are on the edge of a breakthrough. It will, in fact, be forced upon us by circumstances if we do not make it ourselves. A new content for education as a discipline needs to be made. Already, beginnings can be detected. For example, most of our psychology and certainly all of it that reaches the teacher-training levels—is individual learning psychology with overtones of growth and development. Social psychology—the study of the behavior of people in groups, their responses to mass communications, etc.—has emerged as a separate discipline. Much can be gained by working pertinent material from this important field into teacher education programs.

New philosophies of education need to be created. The recent NSSE Yearbook is rich in suggestions in this matter. All of the remaining social sciences—anthropology, political science, International relations, etc.—can contribute much Experiments in the biology of the mentally retarded, new advances in psychiatry, and the new stress theory of disease can all give a little to the new content in education. We need now to work with experts in these disciplines and get the material flowing into our thinning lifeblood that still carries the weak corpuscles of "life-adjustment" and "purposive activity.' The age of automation will require it.

One final word as to the content of education as a discipline. Much has been heard in recent years from critics of education, such as Arthur Bestor that, "there ain't no such thing" as a content in education. Bestor's position, of course is untenable. However, it has, no doubt, been true that some courses in education have been sadly lacking in the content that was there fro the asking. The new content that the age of automation suggests will be much more demanding intellectually than that we already have. The problems of teacher education will become, therefore, more acute No true profession in the age of automation will be able to slough off its intellectual obligations.

7

Printed Materials in the Classroom

Printcd matcrials are one of the oldest and most widely used forms or educational resources. They include books, pamphlets, magazines and newspapers, and single sheets, Printed materials can be distinguished from other forms of media by the fact that they are composed or leaves or sheets on which information is displayed in rows of characters or symbols. Visual material such as line drawings, halftones, graphs and the like may tic interspersed within these rows as well. Some printed materials are only a single sheet in length, while others contain a number of sheets that are folded stitched, glucd, tied, bound, or stapled together along one side to form a sort of packet. Printed materials can be issued in single or multiple copies; the production of multiple copies is accomplished by means of either the printing or the photoduplication processes, However, printed materials are frequently combined with other forms of media to form multimedia packages, which may be either locally or commercially produced. In the United Kingdom, facsimiles of historical documents are often combined with other related materials to create integrated packages for use in the teaching of history.

Advantages and disadvantages

In an instructional setting, printed materials fulfil a dual function: as a medium of communication and as a medium of instruction. The advantages of printed materials in these two modes tire several, Printed materials permit a reader to skim their contents and to react spontaneously to them by making marginal comments or underlining, They can be produced in multiple copies, and can thus be used for independent Study. They will tolerate delays in completion; a reader can stop, put the material away, and return later to the point of termination. Because they allow a reader to return again and again to the same point, print materials facilitate the study of difficult or complicated concepts, They are easily portable, and do not require expensive or complicated to be consulted. If produced in it loose-leaf or ring binder format, they can be quickly and easily revised and updated. Most importantly, they are a familiar formal lo teachers and students alike. At the same time, however, printed materials possess some disadvantages. They cannot present motion materials effectively as a result, their ability to engage all of our senses for a total learning experience is quite limited.

They are also difficult to revise and update if produced in a hardbound format.

Books

A book is a written or printed work, produced and issued as an independent unit, and generally more than 50 pages in length. It may be composed solely of printed material, or it may contain a mixture of visual and textual elements. If the visual material functions merely to decorate or enhance the text, the book is called an illustrated book, If the illustrations carry the essence of the book's meaning, however, it is termed a picture book, Types of books commonly found in today's classrooms are picture books, textbooks, workbooks, paperback books, and reference books. Before beginning any course of instruction involving books, students need to become familiar with the parts of a book, These include the cover (binding and spine), the preliminary materials, the body (main text and illustrations), and the supplementary materials (appendix, bibliography, glossary, footnotes, and index). Students also need to learn how to use a book, which implies understanding the book's structure, the kinds or information it contains, and how to retrieve information from it.

Picture books

Picture books are a special type of modern book in which visual and textual material are of' equal importance, They are of two kinds: true picture books and picture storybooks, In true picture books, illustrations appear on nearly every page and tire closely synchronized with the text. Examples include, alphabet books, counting books, shape and colour recognition books, and books designed to help identify abstractions or concepts such as time, distance, mass, or size. In picture storybooks, text and illustrations form a unified presentation, with both being used to tell a continuing story and convey changes in mood, setting, and plot and character development.

In selecting picture books, three elements should be considered: the text, the illustrations, and the graphic presentation. The traditional criteria of literary analysis are used in the evaluation of picture-book texts. Illustrations may be judged, by whether their style is appropriate to the mood of' the text, whether they are accurate and authentic in detail, and whether they form a harmonious unit with the textual material. Criteria advocated for the evaluation of a book's graphic presentation include consideration of the appropriateness and effectiveness of its size, cover and jacket design, type face, paper quality, and arrangement of printed and visual material.

Traditionally, picture books have been designed for use with young children, but recently 'picture books intended for young adult and even adult readers have been produced. With young children, picture books can be used to aid in concept or object recognition, to develop vocabulary and language skills, to build cultural or literary awareness, and to answer questions about the world around us, Picture books can be used with all ages to convey information, to aid in the socialization process, to challenge the imagination, to develop understanding and appreciation of the graphic arts, and is a source of pleasure and enjoyment.

Textbooks

Textbooks are books that are designed to present the basic principles or aspects of a given subject for use as the basis of instruction; they can, in fact, be considered as an entire course of study in print. They are highly organized they contain a summary of a specific body of knowledge, and they usually contain learning activities or suggestions for further study. Although these attributes have contributed markedly to the improvement of modern instruction, they have also provoked severe criticism. Because textbooks are designed to summarize a subject, it is said that they do not encourage in-depth learning. Because they are so highly structured, they may tend to ossify a subject, encouraging rote learning rather than creative inquiry, Because textbooks must be used by many different types of students, they often are not responsive to the needs and abilities of individual learners. Textbooks have also been criticized for the inclusion of racial, ethnic, and sexual stereotypes at odds with Our changing multi-ethnic and multicultural society. Much current research involving textbooks, therefore, focuses on the identification of inappropriate, insensitive, or outdated material.

Although some of the criticisms levelled at textbooks can be traced to content or structural limitations, others are the result of inappropriate or insensitive applications.

Because of this, teachers have a special responsibility to understand the nature of their textbooks and to use them creatively and effectively.

Five basic patterns characterize contemporary textbook utilization. The traditional pattern is to use textbooks as a source of homework assignments, either for reading or various types of exercises. Related to this is the use of textbooks as a source of problems for students to work through on their own—a pattern common in mathematics instruction. Textbooks may be used as the primary source of instruction, allowing their content and structure to determine the nature and arrangement of the course. Two or more textbooks may also be used in conjunction with one another as the basis of instruction. A variation of this is the multitext approach, where a single text is replaced by a classroom collection containing a variety of textbooks. Students functioning in this mode must make use of the classroom textbook collection, but are free to choose the particular text they find most useful. Finally, textbooks can be used as supplementary materials, with reading matter or exercises from them incorporated where appropriate, to expand upon or elucidate materials presented via other instructional means.

Workbooks

In the United States, workbooks are large paperbound books, usually produced on 81 x 11 inch pages and in ring binder or spiral bound format. They are closely associated with textbooks, and many American textbooks are sold together with an accompanying workbook. In the United Kingdom, worksheets or workcards are more common. These are smaller in size, often resemble a pamphlet in nature, and may be either locally or commercially produced. Worksheets and workcards may be linked to textbooks, reference books, or nonfiction books; they can also be used independently for practical activities. Related to workbooks are laboratory manuals, which are similar in physical format to the American workbook, and are used principally in science education.

Workbooks, worksheets, and workcards are designed to provide a collection of objective exercises for the mastery of specific skills, They are highly structured; a typical format includes statements of behavioural objectives, instructions to the user, experiences and activities designed to facilitate skills mastery, and self-evaluation mechanisms.: Laboratory manuals are also highly structured; their function, however, is to provide directions for carrying out a specific procedure or experiment. Thus laboratory manuals commonly include instructions to the, student, statements of objectives to be accomplished, diagrams illustrating correct procedure, and space for recording the outcome of' the process or experiment.

Since workbook function as a source of exercises for skills mastery, the quality of the exercises they contain is critical. The value of workbooks can in fact be measured by the creativeness of the exercises they contain. Other useful criteria for the evaluation of' workbooks include selecting workbooks that have been student tested, that encourage users to think about the skills they are trying to master, that can be used independently, and that are appropriate for use by students of varying needs, interests, and abilities.

Workbooks can be used effectively in a reinforcement mode, in a motivational mode, and to present bilingual or multilingual material. the reinforcement mode is the traditional approach, and involves the use of workbook activities to reinforce student learning of skills that have already been partly mastered. This is frequently seen in English studies classes, where workbook exercises are used to teach correct grammatical structures, The motivational mode incorporates exercises that can be completed successfully, but demand ' a certain amount of creativity, such as designing a machine to complete an absurd activity in order to convey the idea of the relationship between an object's form and its function. Finally, workbooks are well-suited to the provision of multilingual instruction. For classes composed of students speaking more than one language, workbooks can be designed that contain a single set of exercises accompanied by parallel instructions in two or more languages.

Paperbacks

Paperback books are similar to hardcover books except that their outer covering is made of a soft flexible paper material. They are of two kinds: mass-market paperbacks and quality paperbacks. Mass-market paperbacks are generally smaller in size and cheaper than hardbound books, and are distributed through mass-sales outlets such as grocery stores, chain stores, and news stands. Examples of mass-market paperbacks include sentimental romances, Westerns, adventure stories, mysteries, formula sports stories, and movie and television tie-ins. Quality paperbacks vary in size, but often approach the dimensions of hardbound books; in addition, they are more expensive than mass-market paperbacks. Quality paperbacks are distributed mostly through bookstores and mail-order book clubs and include reprints of classics and out-of-print titles, original works, collections of readings on issues or themes, anthologies of poetry or prose, and paperback editions of hardcover textbooks.

There are three patterns common to the instructional use of contemporary paperbacks. They are used in the teaching of reading, either as reading motivators or as resources for the development of specific reading skills.

Mass market paperbacks have been found to be ideal reading materials for the reluctant reader because they seem less forbidding than hardbound books, they possess highly illustrated covers that are attractive to Students, they are less expensive than other types or books, and they often deal with topics of' more immediate interest to contemporary students. Quality paperbacks can be used to sensitize students to contemporary world problems. Many of the quality paperbacks currently available deal with major social issues and concerns, such as the arms race, world peace, world hunger, drug addiction, consumer fraud, race relations, or environmental issues, Paperbacks dealing with topics such as these can form the basis of sensitive classroom discussion and analysis. Finally, both mass-market paperbacks and quality paperbacks are used as supplementary materials. Another instructional medium, such as a textbook, is used to present basic concepts or skills, while paperbacks furnish examples or illustrations of these concepts or skills in use.

Reference books

Reference books are a form of book designed to be consulted for a specific piece of information rather than to be read through from cover to cover. They contain large numbers of facts organized for use, and may be' arranged alphabetically, chronologically, or topically. There are two types of reference books: those which contain the needed information and those which tell the user where information can be found. Collections of reference books are found in school libraries or media centers and in classroom collections maintained by individual teachers. Reference books commonly found in a classroom collection include an unabridged dictionary, a general encyclopedia, an atlas, and a general almanac.

One of the aims of modern education is to help

students improve their ability to find and use information. Teachers have an obligation, therefore, to see that students receive instruction in the effective use of reference books. Such instruction, which may be termed use of reference books, library or research skills, or use of information sources, is frequently presented jointly by the teacher and the school library media specialist. Instruction in the use of reference books involves helping students recognize the kinds or reference books available, the types of questions or information needs a person may have, and how to select the appropriate reference source for the question being studied. Effective reference book utilization also entails study of the characteristics of a reference book, such as its purpose and objectives, how it is arranged, the nature of its entries, the types of study aids it provides, the cross-reference and index structure, the type of bibliographies provided, and any special features it may possess.

From the viewpoint of curriculum planning, instruction in the use of reference books should be presented systematically throughout a student years of schooling. An ideal sequence would begin with picture dictionaries in kindergarten and the first year; selected handbooks, manuals, geographical dictionaries, and periodical indexes in the second and third years; abridged and unabridged dictionaries, general and subject encyclopedias, maps, atlases, and almanacs ill the fourth and fifth years; yearbooks and biographical dictionaries in the sixth, seventh, and eighth years; and foreign language dictionaries, thesauruses, and specialized indexes in the ninth, tenth, eleventh and twelfth years. In such a system, instruction in the use of a particular type of reference book will be repeated and expanded in higher grade levels in order to reinforce student learning.

Pamphlets

Pamphlets are unbound independent': publications, generally of less than 50 pages. They may be issued singly or in series. Pamphlet materials focus upon a single subject, but may vary widely in topic, size, and format. They may be issued by private businesses, government agencies, educational units, and social and professional organizations; they may also be home or locally produced. As instructional materials, pamphlets have several advantages. They are compact, they are usually less expensive that' other types or printed materials, they are highly current, and they often treat topics that are too narrow or specialized to be dealt with in book form.

In schools having a central library or media center, collections of pamphlets relevant to the total school curriculum will be obtained by the library or media center and housed in a special pamphlet or vertical file collection. Individual teachers, however, frequently maintain their own collections of pamphlets for use as supplementary classroom materials. Example of the types of pamphlets that might be included in either a library media center or individual classroom collection are: government publications; trade catalogues; college and technical school catalogues; annual reports of businesses, organizations, or government agencies; reprints of magazine or journal articles; transcripts of radio or television programs; newsletters from businesses, associations, government agencies, or chambers of commerce; and travel leaflets and brochures. Newspaper and magazine clippings or cuttings are often included here as well.

Newspapers and magazines

Newspapers and magazines are two forms of printed periodical publications. They are published in successive parts, at regular intervals, and are generally designed to be issued oil a more or less indefinite basis. Newspapers are most apt to appear on a daily or weekly schedule; magazines at weekly, monthly, or quarterly intervals. Often a distinction is made between a magazine and a journal.

Modern newspapers and magazines contain a mixture of four types of material: informational and/or news materials, entertainment features, guidance materials, and advertising, Newspapers and magazines possess a number of features that make them ideal instructional materials. They are very current, and contain a vast amount of material on contemporary issues. They are economical, and readily available in multiple copies. They are a form of publication that is familiar to modern students. They are a never-ending source of bulletin board, display, or scrapbook material, and they provide valuable material for clipping or cuttings files

Newspapers and magazines are used in the classroom in two different ways. One pattern is to teach about the publication; the other is to teach with it. Teaching about a newspaper entails a study of how a newspaper is produced and constructed, who is responsible for it, and what it contains.

8

Film, Television and Video

The increasing prominence of moving picture images in our society are the impact of technological change on the production and distribution of those images; and the significance of new kinds of relationship between producer and consumer.

One major change is that definitions of "film," "television,' and "video" have begun to overlap, "Film", or "cinema," continues to be identified with large screen theatre systems as well as nontheatrical and classroom; systems: and with collective audience in schoolrooms, auditoria, and theaters. "Television" is equated with network, studio, and national broadcasting systems, including cable and satellite transmission. The term 'video" while used interchangeably with television, is becoming more applicable to mobile, flexible, creative electronic productions, and is also distinguished from mobile, flexible motion picture productions usually made on 16mm film. The technical distinctions, however, seem to blur. What the world is, or seems to be, at any given moment is increasingly dependent upon what people see and hear in the form of mediated experiences. The ubiquity of film and television, in particular, is changing the very nature or knowledge or, at least, the process of cognition. What was once easily identified as "fiction," or "fact" or "education" or "entertainment" has now become more difficult to distinguish. Everywhere in the world people ire becoming more dependent upon these captured images, and there are some who already feel uncomfortable witnessing a live event without also being able to view it in close-up from several angles, with immediate playback in slow-motion or in freeze frame form. Much of what is happening in a kaleidoscopic world is so rapid, abstract, and changing that the only way to understand it seems to be through the encapsulation, reorganization, and interpretation found on some kind of photoelectronic screen.

The result is the production and delivery of an increasing amount of everyday information for business, military, government, science, arts, humanities, and education through photoelectronic imagery found in industrial plants, business offices, barracks, laboratories, community centers, classrooms—and in homes, Such uses expand the traditional pattern of film and television production to match the requirements of a greater variety of specific audiences or learners, emphasizing modular structure, operational simplicity, accessibility, adaptability to related but different media systems, and interactive qualities to engage the viewer directly in the teaching learning process. The latter attribute, in particular, makes the consumer or "prosumer" of mediated message systems a part of the image-making process itself since lie or she may after the rate and succession of images at will, thus changing the nature of the production itself.

At the same time the use of conventional film and television production and distribution methods continues to be important in educational systems everywhere. In 1981 in the United States, the 16mm film was still the medium preferred by teachers in fields such as home economics, agriculture, career guidance, science, and technological areas, and more than a million 16mm sound film projectors were in use in schools, colleges, universities, churches, and industrial training programs. The 35mm and 16mm film systems remain among the most standardized technologies while electronic systems are typically incompatible. However, in the late 1980s videocassettes became the common denominator in instructional and home media environments.

Forecasts vary about the state of media technology in the year 2000, but it should be remembered that, with the exception of photography, all of the "new" photoelectronic media of communication have been fully developed only within the span of a single human lifetime. In the perspective of history, modern-day humans are still the primitives, writing on the walls of modern-day caves, creating lights and sounds with media that the still being invented.

As new technologies develop, dire predictions of the demise of earlier forms also appear. However, photography did not replace painting; the motion picture did not replace the book; television did not kill radio or the film. No medium has ever destroyed any other medium but rather has brought about shifts, in the functions of each, In the 1980s more print materials were being produced than ever before, radio wits very active tit every part of the world, and while the number of large-budget motion pictures was down, thousands, of low-budget films of all types were being produced, and videotape formats of several kinds were used to produce both professional and amateur video productions, Yet 8mm film is still used in teaming systems, 9.5mm is still used by a few amateur, in Europe, and 9.75mm is in wide use lit educational and informational programs in the People's Republic of China.

In 1981, 41 percent of all television programming in the United States originated on film. In "prime time" this reached 80 percent due to the heavy use of feature films and films made specifically for television. Both television and film studios are being built around the world, and film processing laboratories are still doing work for both film and television industries. The Finnish Broadcasting Corporation began operating a l6mm color laboratory in 1979 capable of processing three million meters of film per year, primarily for television news, In Denmark in 1983, television film was still being processed, although most news for television was on tape or ENG—Electronic News Gathering.

In addition to great advances in electronic technology, photographic innovations continue to be made. In 1982, Eastman Kodak introduced a 35mm color negative film with an exposure index of 1000, making it possible to make pictures under nearly, any existing light conditions. The Fuji Corporation introduced an improved 8mm film that year, and similar developments were seen in motion picture cameras, lenses, lighting equipment, and sound recording and: playback systems,

Films are extensively used at Disney's Experimental Prototype Community of Tomorrow (EPCOT), in Florida, including a 3-D animation production with twin 70mm projectors which throw images onto a 55-foot screen. Another exhibition uses five interlocked projectors and 100 screens of different dimensions, forming a 195-foot master mosaic—each screen being controlled by a microprocessor which makes if possible to move each individually in several positions in 30-degree increments. The entire audience may also be rotated 180-g on a moving platform, bringing the viewers from a film experience to a "live" performance: instigated by the preceding motion picture. "Zones of smell" are also included, using a powerful airgun to deliver and exhaust appropriate odors to supplement the visual experience. The Canadian and the People's Republic of China pavilions both use two complete 180 projections with films of large format. The French display also using large format films, was transferred to videocassette for synchronous, digital editing purposes. Such combinations of film and video technology are improving the quality and efficiency of audiovisual productions. This is especially true in film-to-tape and tape to-film transfers, utilizing high-definition electronic systems with scanning specifications of 60 fields per second with 1,125 scanning lines interlaced 2:1. The trend is for producers to use motion picture technology for original productions, especially on location—that is, in the field—because of its flexibility and convenience, and then transfer the photographic images to videotape for editing and postproduction work. The result is transferred to film where 16mm or 35mm prints are required.

While the present television and video transmission standards of, 525 lines and 625 lines are not adequate to reproduce either the vertical or horizontal high resolution of 35mm and 70mm film, high-definition video for home reception is an expected development before the end or the century. This would make possible large-screen television originating on either film or videotape, with a 1,125-line system producing detailed images such as scientific or mathematical information and print as well as fine art work and graphics, projected on large classroom screens as well its on small theater screens.

An interesting aspect of' the synergism between film and videotape is the apparent resurgence of the "kinescope" and "telecine" —early forms of recording and playing back a television program on film before the advent of videotape. Improvements in this process, the continued use of film for original production, and a vast backlog of film-based material has resulted in the growth of telecine usage in postproduction facilities. In the London area in 1983, over 60 such telecines were operative in addition to 50 in use throughout the British Broadcasting Corporation.

A " teleproduction" of the twenty-first century may begin with a camera crew shooting with electronic cameras where the images are formed on nonsilver halide surfaces composed of organic implants embedded in the material itself. In 1982 Eastman Kodak developed such a photographic film with a magnetic coating on the non-sensitive side which provided machine-readable information for nearly every postproduction situation, coded for immediate, detailed identification of every kind. Combination cameras, designed with the best attributes or cinema usage and the best of electronic camera features will be digital, have no moving parts, use diffraction, rather than refractive optics, and be greatly reduced in bulk, weight, and complexity. If the shots are made on location, or in the field, the actors, special effects, and computer generated animation may be added in the postproduction Studio and colors will not only be corrected, but added or subtracted with precision, and the final editing will be electronic. The final master copy will be transferred to film using a laser scan or an electronic beam to produce prints for conventional screening situations. For worldwide release first-run showings, the master videotape will be transmitted to special theaters or to homes by Direct Broadcast Satellite. Copies will be available in several formats of videotape, or videodisc, or in the form of solid-state information chips or cubes which, when ultimately accessible in volume, may be had at a cost which would make illegal duplication uneconomic.

"Electronic cinema," a term popularized by filmmaker Francis Ford Coppola, begins with the keying of' the script into a word processor, making possible almost instantaneous print-out of the many changes in a motion picture or television script. An "electronic storyboard" is developed by transferring sketches of each scene to a videodisc. A similar "audio sketch" is made of the actor's dialogue, the sound effects, and the music which are also added to the videodisc, providing it complete pre-visualization of the total production which makes possible changes and Improvements in direction, lighting, performance, camera set-ups, sound, editing, and other elements before the actual production begins.

It was predicted by the supervisor of Coppola's Electronic Cinema Division at his Zooetrope Studio that:

> The next important development would be to enable our illustrators to draw straight onto the system with a light pen, and then connect that to the script via a word-processing unit. Eventually, we'll have a giant database, so that you can point with a light pen to a section of the script, and if you're a financial guy, the system will give you the budgetary information; if you're an editor, it can call up the relevant image: if you're a designer, you call recall your blueprints and dimensions. Our ultimate aim is high-definition video, which will take the film out of filmmaking altogether.

Preproduction planning, testing, and prototyping is not new to the field of educational and instructional film production, much work in this dimension having been done in industry and military audiovisual programs during the Second World War and afterwards in universities. This also included psychometric testing on sample audiences of intended learners and experimental work on nearly every aspect of film production. What is new is the application of computer-based visual, audio, and word-processing systems which make multiple-factor analysis easier and quicker to accomplish. Whether such methods will be affordable in education is questionable, the cost of maintaining and replacing the high technology involved in computer-based production is often not Included in production cost statements.

This raises the interesting and very real possibility

that "high" technology will not completely replace "low" technology, the latter being more "appropriates" than the former in many educational settings throughout the world. What Ivan Illich refers to as "convivial tools," as contrasted with those which may be used only by experts, would include simple spring-driven 16mm cameras and half-inch and quarter-inch videotape equipment in cassette forms in systems small enough to combine both recorder and camera with a two-hour tape capacity and instant playback format. By 1904 Eastman Kodak had developed a combination electronic quarter-inch camera and playback system using videotape cassettes.

The accessibility of such equipment will put the means for image production into the hands of more people, professionals and amateurs alike, than ever before in history. The implications of this development for leaching and !earning are treated in a later section in terms of producer-consumer synergism. The question of the relationship between film, television, and video production seems most reliably answered by observing that both photographic and electronic forms will continue to exist and improve in increasingly intricate and mutually supportive combinations. But the principles of communication and the central importance of the design of such productions for educational, informational, and entertainment purposes will be of continuing concern, regardless of the specific and changing photoelectronic technologies involved.

Design in film and television for education

"Design" may be defined its the thoughtful, artful, organic application and creative control of a learning experience. It provides a flexible but purposeful framework for a film or television production which, while carefully planned with the nature of the learner and the instructional objectives clearly in mind will stimulate and energize the learner's own imagination, judgment, and abilities whether the material or content be in the cognitive, psychomotor, or affective domain. An ideal educational production would be one which would serve in this capacity for both teacher and learner, providing a rich experience which could be shared. That many entertainment programs, both film and television, are experienced in this way by large segments of the population, young and old, is a fact which should be studied by designers and producers of educational media.

After more than 60 years of film research, however, there is very little evidence that much ' of it hits been either really helpful, or widely applied. Many studies have been taken from behavioural science models, most deal with cognitive processes, and new research methodologies which explore the affective domain have yet to be developed by educational researchers. The effects of the public media have been widely reported and much publicized, usually with negative conclusions, but little of such information has been employed to improve the design and production or film and television programming either for theaters, broadcast, or for educational productions. A singularly grim picture or the future of instructional design and development is painted by some educational media specialists:

> What can we expect in the area of designing instruction? Unfortunately, I see little of profound importance occurring in the next few years. It would appear that we are continuing to plow the same worn ground in learning theory. While research on lateral specialization of the brain holds some promise, I personally doubt it will have it major near-term influence on how we design instruction. Similarly, our models of the instructional development process show little prospect of soon

> leading us to any brave new world. Almost no significant conceptual advances have occurred in these models in the last few years and I predict none in the near future.

Educational systems continue to lag behind other sectors of society for well-identified academic, economic, and, political reasons. Large-format film and television, for example, arc infrequently round in educational settings, On the contrary, classrooms and school auditoria are typically inadequate if not deplorable even in the simplest l6mm seating, auditory, and projection requirements, "Spectator comfort" has been a principal concern of the CSTCF—the *Commission Superieur Technique du Cinema Francais*—for at least a decade, and the Society of Motion Picture and Television Engineers has published long-established standards tor film and television viewing situations, but the recommendations of such internationally recognized bodies seem to be ignored by educational administrators in designing learning environments.

The media arc changing the nature of such environments, including the home, and the function of the teachers as well. Teachers are referred to as "providers" in the Canadian Teledon cable system. A new abbreviated way of writing is required for the print messages in teletext material on the television tube raising questions of legibility, rate of delivery, vocabulary level, and other issues once thought to be only the province of print, "Visual literacy" is coming to have a meaning that must include reading as well as visual abilities. The essential function of print is thus subsumed in the total design of what have been classically characterized as media which have undermined the young learner's ability and interest in the book.

The design of educational materials is affected by the parsimony of television messages, including the commercials, as well as by the longer, multi-episode television series and miniseries. Such design must take into account the likelihood of individual ownership of visual materials in the form of videotapes and videodiscs. This will make possible the random accessing and comparative personal viewing of film and television programs which were formerly only available in group settings.

Good design in educational productions has always included the elements of organization, amplification or enhancement of the subject, simplification, and dramatization. Today, media designers are also concerned with the elements of flexibility, modularity, and interaction with the viewer or learner,

Open systems such as videotex add other dimensions to the educational potential of the electronic media. For example, when using the Prestel system in the United Kingdom, and Antiope in France, a consumer—learner is hooked up to telephone lines or coaxial cable linked to a television receiver with which he or she can interact with or instruct the machine by using a calculator-type keyboard. In Columbus, Ohio, the Warner QUBE system provides 30 channels with five response buttons making possible, through connection with a home computer, interactive exchanges between the studio and the viewers including political polling, game shows, and credit courses at three educational institutions in the area. This system however, once extended to several other cities has been found economically unviable, and interactive programming was greatly reduced by 1984. A more sophisticated interactive experiment is found in a community in Japan where all households oil the system have direct, interactive cable communication with respondents in all other households in the system. While presently mostly used for person-to-person communication, the potential for the use of film, videotape, and videodisc materials in these settings may begin to be realized as respondents on these interactive systems explore ways to visualize as well as verbalize their messages. Visual contact through built-in cameras or videophone systems linked to disc, tape, or film playbacks could produce, in homes and schools, the effect now found in teleconferencing in industry and business settings and in some university or public broadcast systems.

Highly creative imagery may be eventually fed into such a system, including some poetic and personal visions in the form of the modern equivalent of the family photographic album, the "snapshot," or the "home movie." References may also be drawn from on-shelf videotapes or videodiscs, selected through random access, to illustrate a point to stimulate those to whom the message is directed to say: "I see what you mean!"

Image consumer as producer

From time of birth all people are image consumers absorbing verbal, visual, and auditory signs and symbols as part of their cultural heritage. But people also continually process such information through their own perceptual system, altering these messages and reproducing them in terms of what they are and what they know. Thus, a great number of factors external to any specific film or television display come into play as part of its effect on any given set of viewers.

The classic transaction between the image maker (communicator) and image consumer (receiver) is immensely enhanced through technology which makes it possible for the viewer to change a given message, not only psychologically but also physically, and to do this instantaneously while a program is in progress. Interactive cable networks offer viewers multiple choices on many issues including what and when certain programs are preferred, which should be cut off before completion, polling of opinion oil public matters, and the like, thus making it possible to receive, collate, and report such reactions on the screen within five seconds, as in the case of the Warner-Amex QUBE system once found in several cities in the United State.

More direct involvement in production has been possible with 8mm film, home videotape recording eqipment, and public broadcast access to the facilities for the creation and public exhibition of film and to works by individuals or civic groups. Thus in the former "Challenge for Change" program in Canada and the present "Public Access" cable channels in the United States, programs conceived and produced by nonprofessionals with the help of experienced broadcast personnel have been put on the air.

While professional producers will always be required, there is a growing involvement of nonprofessionals in the image-making process. A large part or this development has been due to the advent of what Illich refers to as "convivial tools" which, as lie defines them,

> ...are those which give each person who uses them the greatest opportunity to enrich the environment with the fruits of his or her vision....Tools foster conviviality to the extent to which they can be easily used by anybody, as often or is seldom as desired, for the accomplishment of a purpose chosen by the user. The use of such tools by one person does not restrain another from using them equally. They do not require previous certification by the User, Their existence does not impose any obligation to use them. They allow the user to express his meaning in action.

This concept is supported by the fact that students are becoming involved in the design and construction of learning materials, from books to films. Amateur videotapes of disasters and other happenings are beginning to appear with more regularity oil both local and network news in the United States and elsewhere, Local cultural 'and ethnic groups are expressing themselves in their own idiom—the Navajo Indians of the American southwest, and the natives of Liberia and Zambia reflecting their own cultural values in film and video forms. The Innuit of northern Canada have their own television station, and the Aboriginals of Western Australia their own radio broadcast facility.

The case for local production is expressed by the chairman of' the public service commission of New Guinea:

> It is a political reality that television will come to Papua, New Guinea. Certainly I have no wish to deprive my fellow Countrymen of the value of good television broadcasting, [but]... we should be doing everything humanly possible to ensure that our television programmes should have a preponderance of locally-made material, scripted and filmed by our own people for our own people.

The same opinion is reflected by the Secretary-General of the South Pacific Commission:

> I think the greatest need is I'm the recognition Pacific cultures, the recognition of the need for Pacific content in radio, television, and film programmes, and hence a need for Pacific professionals in the industry.

In 1982 at the 21st International Congress or the Centre Internationale de Liasion des Ecoles de Cinema et de Television, representatives of national film and television schools from more than 30 nations passed a resolution that students of cinema and television production should be trained and educated to communicate not only with audiences of theatrical films and broadcast television, but also for purposes of education, information, and national development. It was declared necessary to combine the study or film, television, and video along with other related communication technologies in courses of study. It was also agreed that the education and training of film and television personnel in the developing countries should receive the support of established training centers who should help such countries to organize their own film and television centers to educate their own producers, and determine the introduction of the appropriate technologies of communication to meet the objectives of their national development.

Such developments appear to be predictive of the future of the film and television producer and the role of the media. It does not seem to restrict, but rather expand, the responsibility of the professional even as production opportunities become more available to the non-professional, since participation in the image production process makes it more collaborative, democratic, and personal as people begin to speak directly to other people through audiovisual imagery.

Futures in media

Forecasting, regarded with suspicion in most academic circles, is a central concern in the communication industry. The Rand Corporation, for example, developed the "Delphi" technique, one of many methodologies being used to reduce bias and the "crystal ball" effect in futuring. For film and television production such futuring is regarded as essential for its existence.

A Delphi study conducted in 1979-80, in 20 countries involving 80 authorities, 21 percent of whom were from universities and international communication institutes, 21 percent from governments and international organizations, 19 percent from aerospace and telecommunications industries, and others from various research organizations, predicted with more than 50 percent agreement, that by the year 2000: there would be continual and rapid growth in the tele-informational services including videotext and videoconferencing; and direct broadcast satellite services in homes for under 100 dollars in the countries associated with the OECD—the Organisation for Economic Co-operation and Development.

Industrialization and the construction of mega-structures in space would be counterbalanced by "a lack of significant progress in achieving unified international, social, political, and economic cooperation in tele-communications or space applications. Global cooperation was thus expected to continue on art ad hoc, piecemeal basis". The summarizer of the report concludes that there would be: "A prosperous and information-rich society, one that risks information overload for its citizenry and in which individual privacy may be endangered by universal data bases and electronic monitoring".

A similar Delphi study conducted in 1981 at Indiana University, exploring the question of the future of film and video specifically in education, reported the consensus of 56 experts in the production of instructional media, including the following predictions: there will be mate emphasis on planning and evaluation as part of production development; media designers and producers by 2001 will be skilled in both technology and instructional design, and will work as teams of technical, creative, and educational specialists; and media design will become more creative, flexible, and interactive with programs being produced with specific objectives for specific learners in both formal and informal learning environments. Referring; to the latter, this report stated that "a major portion of the instructional media of 2001 will be used in the home; an increase in leisure time will result in a greater demand for instructional materials for the general public; the home market will be the driving force for the development of instructional hardware and software; and that the development of the home market will make possible the mass distribution of instructional media at low cost".

The role of commercial producers of educational media is seen as "critical" by some educators because "Teachers don't know enough about designing varied forms of instruction". Interactive cable, educational conferencing by satellite, high-definition video and videodisc, and even "talking toys" are identified as being the significant media of the future. On the other hand, there' seems to be little emphasis on advances in matters of instructional design and development although considerable research may be devoted to these areas.

The evidence on the future of the role of media, as in other forecasting, is mixed, but it appears that an immense quantity of photoelectronic production will be needed to satisfy the requirements of entertainment, instruction, and education in the decades ahead to meet a sustained growth in the number of persons having access to such media. In this process the rivalry between film and television technologies will become obsolete as they merge and become interrelated with the microcomputer, telephone, and other communication technologies.

The historic fear of the negative influence of film and television may also be demystified as more consumers and groups of consumers become aware of the ways in which these media are constructed and as they continue to gain access to the means of production. A French communications expert at a UNESCO conference in Paris expressed this recent optimistic vision: "I do not know what type of happiness is given to people without television, but I know all the pleasure I have to get all the knowledge of this world by pushing just a button, and I feel very lucky to have this strange window 24 hours a day in my living.

Production of photoelectronic media of the future must be based on designs that take into account their uses in "24-hour living" environments in it proliferation of forms including videodisc, tape, film, cable television, satellite transmission, 360° screens to be seen by thousands of viewers at one time, and screens the size of a wrist watch for an audience of one.

More and better trained designers and producers are needed, including professional groups utilizing "high" technologies, its well its local, indigenous individuals and groups who will continue to make useful and successful productions using less expensive "low" technologies Producers of all types will need to have some form of continuing education to keep tip with rapidly shifting technology and the changing needs of education and society. Producers, working with educators, will need to participate in media futuring, although the predictions as referred to in earlier citations mention technologies which, for the most part, are already in place, and there are very few surprises in these forecasts. There will be a continual increase in the number and kinds of photoelectronic productions and, in an information-rich world society, there will always be some groups and individuals who will be more and better informed than others. Worldwide communication systems being implemented by international corporations may or may not equalize educational opportunities for all. Quantity of production and multiplication of delivery system forms does not mean a quantum leap in the improvement of quality, unless educators, teachers, administrators, designers, and media producers place the highest priority on the development of a world population of verbally and visually literate human beings. This requires massive administrative, financial, and human resources devoted to the design, production, and utilization of all forms of these proliferating photoelectronic media for the purpose of teaching the world the things which must be known to relieve the pressing personal, national, and international problems shared by all, and to improve the quality of entertainment, education, and life itself in the twenty-first century.

9

Use of Television in the Classroom

This chapter deals mainly with the systematic use of instructional television programs in elementary and secondary classrooms. Other uses are treated elsewhere. A historical introduction leads to a discussion of roles for classroom television and hence to patterns of use. Many countries that adopted classroom television in the late 1950s and early 1960s had already had some experience with classroom radio. Educators had seen the benefits of using electronic mass media to bring stimulating materials from the world at large into the classroom. Television broadcasters, like their radio predecessors, saw school programming as a good opportunity to render an important and necessary public service. Yet what seemed to be a mutually satisfactory relationship was in many instances an uneasy alliance. Educators were concerned mainly with pedagogical values, whereas broadcasters, focusing on the medium, were concerned mainly with entertainment and audience appeal.

The pattern of development was markedly different in North America and Europe. North American initiatives were primarily local and usually ambitious. Encouraged the extravagant claims of proponents of new media, school administrators looked on television as a means of improving curricula, of upgrading teachers, and of bringing about significant changes in educational practice. Teachers, on the other hand, often looked on classroom television as an imposition from above and as a threat to their long-cherished sense of autonomy. They resented the implication that their teaching was somehow deficient, and they found repugnant such terms as "follow-up teacher" or "receiving teacher." They further resented the inflexible broadcasting schedules, which made little allowance for individual needs.

Many teachers, along with administrators, were appalled by the quality of most of the early programs. Television had been promoted as a "window on the world," a "magic box," and so forth, but in fact it offered too many programs of' "talking heads" teachers standing in front of chalkboards, giving conventional lectures in a conventionally didactic manner. By the late 1960s, however, educators and broadcasters started moving in more productive directions. Each group made greater efforts to understand the other's Point of view, with the result that classroom television became, often, a product of cooperation and integration built from creative tension rather than from antagonism and mistrust.

The quality problem was less marked in Europe where production was in the hands of national broadcasting agencies. However, the development of classroom television was quite slow. There was little pressure oil teachers to use the television programs available, and many education authorities were apprehensive of the cost of progressively equipping all their schools. Although a minority of teachers were enthusiastic from the outset, many were unwilling to adapt their teaching to accommodate the new medium. They felt unsure of themselves in handling it, and scheduling was a major source of difficulty in most secondary schools.

The producers, meanwhile, had been experimenting with pilot schemes and were learning what television could most usefully and effectively provide for the classroom. In the United Kingdom, where the term used was always educational rather than instructional broadcasting ' the first television programs were almost exclusively directed to the enrichment both of children's experiences and of their teachers' resources. In the secondary schools, which were their first target, both the British Broadcasting Corporation (BBC) and the independent television companies endeavoured by means of a varied output in such subjects as geography, science, current affairs, and drams to add a dimension of their own to the teacher's work. In spite or the difficulties of time-tabling and the priority generally given by teachers to their own basic courses and television often being referred to as a frill, these enrichment programs acquired a faithful and appreciative clientele sometimes: of considerable size. Talking heads were an infrequent source of complaint, and programs were valued for the skilful application of studio techniques, a wide ranging use of film, and a generally high standard of performance.

In the primary schools the flexibility of the curriculum made it easier for teachers to adopt television as a stimulus to their work and as a springboard for interesting new projects. The visual element soon became immensely popular, making conspicuous contributions over a wide field of general knowledge in music and in remedial work. Eventually some series; attracted audiences in 70 or even 80 percent of junior and infant schools.

In contrast to developed countries, developing countries have seen the emergence of different problems as they have attempted to use television in classrooms. Since the early 1970s, developing countries have devoted enormous resources to education. Because of the expense of developing a traditional Western school system, administrators turned to technology in an effort to do more with fewer teachers and at the same time to take advantage of the economics of scale associated with broadcasting.

Although more planning has been in done in recent years, at first many groups rushed in too quickly. Weaknesses in curriculum and instructional planning became widely evident in short order. Plans to provide universal quality education through television in it few years were unrealistic, and the several attempts; to do so were unsuccessful. What took a century in Europe and North America could not be done in it year or two.

The belief that television would reduce educational costs was also mistaken. Television still required the presence of a teacher for its most advantageous use. It was an addition to the system and often improved neither the quality nor the quantity of classroom instruction.

Problems similar to those in developed nations also emerged. The teachers who had training, especially at the high-school level, found television programs to be inconsistent with their teaching values and styles. Administrative mandates were not sufficient justifications for the use of television; poorly developed curricula led to teachers' rejection of material. Television was superimposed on the educational system without respect for the nature of the system.

Television should not be blamed for the failures. A medium that promised everything a solution to all of education's problems, a cure for an ailing society, economical and political benefits was not capable of living up to expectations, It is less productive to blame thee medium than to change the expectations.

Classroom television can be highly beneficial to education and society in nations with widely diverse political, economic, and educational systems. In order to succeed, television must do only what it does best.

Roles

Educators who have chosen to adopt classroom television have usually done so for one or more of the following reasons:

Improvement of quality

Ideally, the television programs represent the best educational efforts of curriculum specialists, program designers, audiovisual artists, and broadcasting specialists; the programs incorporate the best, most up-to-date thinking in the field; and the content is presented in an attractive and stimulating format.

Television as a catalyst

Classroom television can also stimulate educators to reconsider curricular options, to evaluate methods of pedagogy now in practice, and to see new relationships among discrete curricular areas. It provides a source of ideas for teachers and can catalyze their development of more varied, more motivating, and more contemporary practices. Classroom television has helped to facilitate the rapid dissemination of new curricular ideas, many of which remain long after their parent projects or programs have been abandoned,

Television as a means of extending children's experience

Television in the classroom is truly what UNESCO has often called it: "a window on the world." The programs allow students to transcend the boundaries of space and time, and to see society in new and diverse ways, The rural child sees life in the city, and the urban child sees life in the country; various patterns of consumption and economic structure, alternative religious forms, cultural patterns, and sexual role models become available.

Television as a means of introducing affective education

Television has been instrumental in introducing affective education into elementary classrooms. Television programs that provide shared, relatively universal experiences have given teachers and students the opportunity to examine their feelings about themselves and their environment. Similar opportunities arise in secondary social studies and humanities. Developing a national identity is an important goal of television in newly independent countries, and television can also be used to encourage and strengthen diverse cultural and religious traditions.

Television as a means of equalizing educational opportunity

Educational inequality is it persistent problem in most countries, from both economic and sociocultural viewpoints. A broadcast signal, however, is not limited to wealthy school districts or to new schools. For young children, in particular, the impact of programs developing basic skills has been encouraging, and similar programs for older students are now being created.

Presenting black faces in all-white schools and white faces in all-black schools provides useful role models of all races to facilitate interracial acceptance and understanding. But what school television can do best in equalizing educational opportunity is to provide instructional presentations so universal that they become specific to every viewer and are effective regardless of sex, race, ethnic background, or economic condition.

Television as a means of improving efficiency and productivity

Productivity in education means significantly more than the ability of fewer teachers to teach more students. It means better preparation of students to be effective and fulfilled members of the community at large. When school television adds to the number of possible approaches to instruction, stimulates improved class interactions, :initiates and reinforces cognitive learning, or motivates better classroom behaviour, it is providing better, more efficient education.

To increase productivity requires finding the right mixture or school television and classroom teaching By using school television economically that is by examining the variety of available utilization and programming options and by choosing wisely educators can effect improvements in the patterns and results of instruction with minimal increases in cost. Television is not seeking to replace teachers, only to assist them in reaching their desired goals.

Television-based instructional systems

In several countries, the main vehicle for achieving some of these goals has been it television-based instructional system. Such systems is ate distinguished, not by their format or purpose, but by their mode of development, The program designers are committed to a method of development that incorporates a student needs assessment, a lesson design, formative evaluation, product revision, summative evaluation, and the revision of objectives and strategies. Their product may include not only television programs but also tiny printed supplementary materials, such as teacher's guides or student workbooks, designed to complement the curriculum directly. The programs are viewed in the classroom on a regular, long-term basis, and should then result either in it measurable difference between the students who receive Instruction by television and those who do not, or in some attributable change over time in learning pain, attitude, or behaviour.

Classroom television must be seen as more than a television program. Complex interactions between the program, people, and their environment all contribute to instruction. To describe the process, it is perhaps easiest to begin with utilization.

Viewing conditions

In some cases, the unit of instruction is the television program alone. Individual viewers learn by themselves, But in most cases, the instructional unit is the television lesson. A teacher spends a few minutes preparing the class, with a series of questions for discussion or independent thought, or a review of previously taught concepts, vocabulary words, or other advance organizers. Then the class attends to the television set and views the program with the teacher.

After the viewing, teachers use a variety of techniques—structured discussions, the teaching of related content written exercises and tests—to continue the lesson. Any activity that reinforces and extends the content will be valuable to students. Sometimes homework, testing, or a long-term project is part of the lesson.

The classroom environment influences the use and the effectiveness of school television. The television receiver must be visible to all students and in good working order; the conditions for transmission and reception or playback must provide a usable signal. The time of day may also be important. Television is a change of pace in a lecture-and-workbook classroom, it may be especially welcome in the late morning before lunch, just after lunch, or in the late afternoon.

Accumulated research evidence suggests that the degree to which the television program becomes part of the traditional classroom process and the degree to which it is treated like other instructional materials, can significantly effect learning. Conversely, the degree to which teachers diminish the perceived value of the program for example, by leaving the room when it is on or by ignoring its content after viewing will determine how credible students find the program.

To use classroom television successfully, one must take into account the nature of the interacting variables: the personal characteristics of teachers and students, the interpersonal relationships within the school and the class, the program itself as designed and produced, and the environmental conditions under which it is viewed.

Teacher

Teachers vary greatly in their ability (and willingness) to develop comprehensive lessons for it television program often they depend on it teacher's guide for the program. Often they take cues from their students and form opinions about the program based on students' reactions to it; a program that holds the attention of the students may be seen as successful even if its content is weak.

Teachers vary also in their attitudes towards television and other technologies in the classroom. If television is presented to them as a means of replacing them or reducing their autonomy, they will use it with great reluctance. However, if television lessons are designed to help meet the learning goals of the classroom, teachers will be quick to adopt and use them. The attitude of administrators also greatly affects the willingness or teachers to use television and the degree of emphasis they place on it. The support system for teachers administrative, technical, student, and parent attitudes also, contributes to successful school television utilization.

Students take cues from their teachers and treat television as they do. However, even if the students bring a positive attitude to the viewing, the program may change their attitude. The program must be at the appropriate development level, must treat the content and the viewer with intelligence, and must appeal to the viewer.

Attention to the television program is a serious concern, While distractions to the viewer at home are common and inconsequential, attention to the program at school is a necessary, though insufficient, condition for learning. Moreover, inattention by a few students can easily escalate if they do something that distracts the teacher and other students.

Instructional design

Research into the nature of viewing and of the viewing audience has led to some understanding of how television works best. The attributes of television programs that contribute to their appeal, salience, interest, and educational value must be insured in the design and production of the programs. The technical resources on command include music, movement, sequencing, format, and character appeal. To make the most of these researchers may often cooperate with designers and producers to create successful programs.

The instructional design of school television programs must also take viewing conditions into' account. If the program is to require no follow-up from the teacher, it should include factors that promote immediate student learning, for example, advance organizers, repetition, and so on. However, if the teacher is to be an integral part of the lesson, the role of the program can be:

(a) to introduce the content for the teacher to elaborate later and to drill the students oil;
(b) to provide background material for a lesson the teacher will deliver;

(c) to reinforce and review ideas already covered in class;

(d) to provide salient illustrations that will stimulate class discussion and discovery.

These pedagogical functions should be taken into account in the design and production of school television programs.

Examples

One well-documented classroom television project is the "Think About" series developed by a consortium of American states and Canadian provinces. The state and provincial education and television agencies received unlimited and unrestricted use or the materials for seven or more years in return for their financial and intellectual support. This series was initiated, developed, and produced over a sixyear period by the Agency for Instructional Television and consists of sixty 15-minute programs for students 10 to 12 years of age.

The project's initial focus was presenting various general problem-solving skills in realistic settings as a means of improving the way students learned and studied. Over the course of the project's development period, the focus shifted towards the reinforcement of already-taught skills in language art social studies, and mathematics. The programs illustrated the application of these subject matter skills in out of school situations. The general problem-solving theme remained in many of the programs but with less emphasis than originally planned. The curriculum was developed in conjunction with leachers and subject matter specialists and extensively verified with classroom teachers.

The design of the programs moved along this path as a result of the influence of the consortium of states and provinces funding the project. The representatives of these funding agencies were, for the most part, middle-level administrators of their state or provincial education or television agency who met regularly during the development and production phases to review programs and reflect on the project's activities. The problem-solving curriculum appeared to them as a drastic departure from the traditional emphasis on subject matter skills and as possibly too advanced for teachers to easily adapt and use in the classroom. The political pressure front the funders resulted in a modification of the curriculum, in a change meant to make the instructional materials more accessible to, and usable by, fifth and sixth-grade teachers.

The television programs themselves are short, realistic dramas that set up a plausible problem for students but end before the problem has been resolved. This approach gains the attention of students by the appeal of the "real-life" drama, and motivates them to finish solving the problem in the classroom. Extensive formative evaluation helped instructional designers identify appealing dramatic segments and salient teaching points. Programs were revised during production based on the feedback provided by representative teachers and classrooms.

The pattern of classroom use is as follows: the teachers focus students' attention on the topic or theme of the program and often relate the theme to ongoing classwork in a specific curriculum. The class and the teacher then view the program together. Following the viewing the teacher directs a discussion of the program, its theme, and the application of ideas presented in the program to activities in school and out. The discussion often takes a spiraling route, at first a recapitulation of the events in the program to be sure everyone understands what has been seen, followed by a generation of alternative hypotheses or solutions to the problem. This is followed, in turn, by relating the problem and its theme to classwork, currently underway. Seatwork assignments and long-term class activities are included in the teacher guide but do not seem to be used frequently.

In use, many teachers find 60 programs to be more than they can comfortably fit into their schedule, especially since they commonly use more than one television series. Thus, alternative utilization patterns have emerged. Rather than using the series at a two-per-week rate over the course of a school year, some teachers, with the cooperation of their broadcasting agencies or with access videocassette recorders, use the first 30 programs foe the fifth grade and the second :30 for the sixth grade. A more common pattern, especially in areas where the use' of videocassette machines is the norm, is the selection and viewing of individual programs or groups of programs oil a common theme when convenient. In this manner the correlation of' the programs with course material is more precise and, because or the foresight and planning required, the television program is very likely to be well-integrated into the lesson.

Evidence from research associated with the "Think About" project shows very modest changes in problem solving abilities, a result due to several Factors, First, measurement of problem-solving skills is an emerging and, exploratory effort with few valid and reliable measures, second, the research design desired by the consortium militated against finding strong experimental-control group differences; and third, the modification of the curriculum placed less emphasis on problem-solving skills, which remained the overall goal of the series. ;Nevertheless, research evidence indicates the widespread appeal and use of the material. The modified curriculum in problem solving—an organised curriculum heretofore not present in more than a handful of classrooms—was adopted and used successfully by a wide variety of teachers who differed greatly in background, teaching style, and subject matter emphasis.

Television Ontario (TVO) has taken a different approach to the development and use of a school television series. TVO is it provincial organization responsible for many aspects of Intraprovince communications Including elementary and secondary classroom television. In contrast to the curriculum development efforts of the Agency for Instructional Television (AIT), which had to find common agreement across state, provincial, and national borders, TVO starts with a centrally adopted curriculum statement and a relatively homogenous population.

To help define educational needs that can best be served by television, discipline-specific advisory committees were formed. These committees periodically commission needs ascertainment surveys or the membership of professional organisations and other teachers of a subjects. These Surveys explore what is taught and what is difficult to teach in exploring the themes that seemed especially difficult to teach, survey results often point to the lack of curriculum support material for those topics.

The discipline advisory committee and TVO staff review the material that is perceived as difficult to teach and partition out those concepts that television would find difficult to do (or that a teacher could do better), and those concepts that are undergoing a change in curricular emphasis and should not be tackled at present. The remaining concepts become a ranked list of priorities.

Two or three practising teachers who teach the subject well work with a TVO producer and writer to develop program materials that can engage teachers and students, remediate the curriculum deficiency, and match the established provincial curriculum.

The "Eureka!" series was developed to meet the needs of seventh and eighthgrade science teachers, usually science generalists, who were having difficulty teaching certain physics topics. The high priority curriculum needs identified by the needs ascertainment survey were all central to the students' understanding of physics and could be directly taught as independent single concepts. The content for short models developed by the 'TVO team was then validated by university faculty and made into single-concept, 5-minute units in full cellanimation. Within this 5-minute unit there were several potential stopping points built in, so that a teacher could have discussion with the class on one aspect of the content, clarify the material, and raise issues for continued focus before continuing the program. This design practically demands the use of videocassettes and about 90-95 percent of the use is with the teacher controlled tape unit. This design also permits the teacher to use the single concept program, follow it with an experiment or book work exercise, and then the class (or individuals within the class) can view the program again.

While the material is designed for in-school use, its highly appealing animation format makes it useful in other contexts. TVO presently use the programs as fillers between science programs during the evening broad casts. The material is widely used and evaluation data are currently being collected to explore its impact.

The "Freestyle" series is a well documented project initiated from a strong federal perspective. These 13 half-hour-long programs were designed to aid children's career development and reduce restrictions on career selection based on sex and social stereotyping. These programs are "prosocial" in their goals and are directed more towards attitude change than towards classroom-related knowledge or behaviour. Nevertheless, these materials found their widest use and greatest impact in the classroom.

This television project was conceived as it major federal initiative to meet broad social goals and its creation was undertaken by a consortium of independent television education, university, and research organizations. Much background research and formative evaluation led to the selection of themes included in the project's curriculum. The mix of educators and "Hollywood" production personnel led initially to great confusion over the amount of instructional content and the degree to which it would be emphasized. A strong executive producer was able to get the production process under control, striking a balance between education and entertainment, with a tilt toward the latter.

The programs were designed with a strong dramatic format and were, structured to balance the highly entertaining material with the social modelling needed to meet educational goals, While initially scripted as half-hour programs, the design called for a dramatic highpoint about halfway through the program. In this format a single program could be divided in two in order to more easily fit classroom time periods. Thus, a half-hour program useful in the broadcast schedule for at home viewing, could be seen in two parts within the same week in a classroom.

As the project was being developed, the influence of the funders and the conflicting demands placed on the producer led to a modification of the project's goals. Rather than give equal focus to racial and gender stereotyping, the emphasis was placed on sexual bias and stereotyping. It was thought that a single major issue could be more easily handled through the format selected. During its first year of availability, a major study of the series impact was conducted on its use at home and in school. Using a best-case model in the schools, the researchers noted impressive changes in attitudes towards nontraditional sexrole behaviour. This best-case model studies the programs under ideal rather than normal conditions of use. Little flexibility is permitted in the manner and amount of viewing and post-viewing activities. Teachers used a warm-up activity to introduce the viewing of the lesson, followed: the class viewing with extensive discussion, and used prepared printed materials for short and long-term follow up.

The impact of the series was reduced under at home conditions and when the emphasis in classrooms was reduced. The setting in which the programs were used and the importance attributed to the instructional nature of the programs seem to have greatly influenced the impact of the series.

The series was widely broadcast to homes and schools during its first year, but its availability diminished rapidly over the next two. It is no longer available since, under the commercially based system of production, the rights to the material were obtained only for three years.

For the 15-year-old school student in the United Kingdom there are some 15 to 20 broadcasts available in any week of the school year. Over half of these are concerned with the main, curricular subjects—mathematics, the sciences, English, history, geography, modern languages. The remainder cover such areas as career guidance, the arts, and social studies. In the latter class the most popular and successful is "Scene," a weekly transmission of documentary or dramatized programs for teenagers, providing material for discussion investigation, and written work.

The introduction and early development of this series is described in some detail by Kenneth Fawdry who was Head of the British Broadcasting Corporation (BBC) Schools Television at that time, and an account by the producer, Ronald Smedley, has also been published. Sonic of the broadcasts are on very controversial topics, and several were specially commissioned scripts from well-known contemporary playwrights. Most are presented from the teenager's angle, with a special thought for the non-intellectual student who is impatient to leave school at 16.

The two descriptions which follow cannot represent the diversity of themes encompassed by "Scene," but they can give some indication of the producer's approach to the audience and of the reactions at the viewing end.

"The Last Bus" tells in dramatized form how a group of high-spirited, irresponsible teenage boys board the last bus home, pick a quarrel with the bus conductor, beat him tip and, as an afterthought, steal his purse. There were a few fellow passengers and, though mildly protesting, none of them came to the victim's aid. The driver, a West Indian, froze to his seat, fearing the consequences to himself and to his family's precarious existence if lie should intervene and himself be mugged in consequence.

A BBC schools' liaison officer reported, after watching the broadcast with a large class of 45 adolescents: "I am convinced they really lived through the whole incident: they had been caught tip in those feelings of devilment, arrogance and hatred that presumably account for many acts of teenage aggression."

Then the scene abruptly changed, The presenter of the program turned investigator and cross-examined each of the passengers as they made excuses for their inaction.

Finally the bus conductor himself showed more magnanimity than the youths deserved, saying that he understood these pranks that got out of hand; he had helped in youth clubs and the like.

Not all the viewing classes appear to have understood this inquisitorial ploy; but, by the crude measuring rod of excited comments and questions afterwards, the program was a spectacular success, Another visiting BBC officer wrote: "This...arresting, provocative but simple story line is a certain way of getting through to this kind of child, who has little reading ability, is bored with traditional teaching.... It may be the nearest they will get to any depth of thought on current social issues."

The following week's broadcast, "The Sentence of the Court," told what happened to the boys and showed the ringleader, very much deflated, in a borstal prison, while a probation officer and a borstal governor were interviewed about their work and spoke frankly about the difficulties and shortcomings of the system of punishment and rehabilitation of which they were a part. This well-devised program did not have the impact of "The Last Bus," but enabled the thoughtful viewer to ponder further the problems of, teenage Violence and its consequences.

The second recent broadcast which also made a considerable impression, "James is our Brother," is a study of a mentally handicapped boy. The program starts with his first unassisted journey home from school—catching the right bus, paying his fare, changing buses, getting off at the right stop a landmark of achievement in James, struggle to cope with the outside world then, his brothers and sisters describe life at home with James, and through copious film inserts is seen gradually surmounting his difficulties, establishing a modus vivendi among his peers, and finally entering for the Olympics for the Disabled and receiving a bronze medal from the Duke or Edinburgh. By now lie is articulate enough to speak for himself and describes his conquest of the problems of everyday life, and lie proudly shows the press photograph of himself with the Duke.

The audience, reaction may be judged from a selection of the postcard reports sent by viewing teachers to the producer of the series:

> Very good because it portrays life from the point of view of' the mentally handicapped person, particularly the last conversation with James. They greatly admired the interviewer's sympathetic handling of James....
>
> The programme was excellent....Many of' the class were very moved. They had been able to appreciate James' gallant attitude to life and his philosophical acceptance of being "different." They noted the maturity of his brothers' attitude, and this led on to discussion led by two pupils who had mongol children in the family....
>
> This outstanding programme...ought, to be a part of every 'school's compulsory studies...

In one school, a class composed a letter to the local council asking for a hostel to be built in file area, and in another school a group of girls decided to offer to help at a nearby school for severely subnormal children.

A BBC schools liaison officer visited a class of 35 boys and girls of good intelligence and watched the taped programme with them, "The atmosphere was electric.... Everyone laughed a lot with James and some of the girls and Hazel (their teacher) were close to tears several times..." Immediately afterwards the teacher got everyone to write down their instant reactions. "Feelings of anger, sadness over the whole situation predominated....The boys were very articulate in expressing their anger at those who laugh at mongols....A group of girls said they didn't realize how human the mentally handicapped feel." They then built up a character study of James and were surprised to find that his qualities and his attitudes were very much like their own. The officer's report goes on to commend the teacher's versa the and imaginative handling of "this superbly moving programme."

Of these four projects, the first three were all developed from carefully researched bases of' information and direction. They differed in the way they related to the educational mission of the schools, "Eureka!" illustrates the closest fit with the existing curricula of schools and was designed to be integrated closely with existing instruction. "Think About" attempted to extend the curriculum slightly by introducing and organizing problem-solving skills. This infusion of new curriculum material succeeded because it built on the familiar, and on the related skills in basic subject areas taught universally in the schools.

"Freestyle," in contrast, attempted to deal with a social problem through instruction. Its initiative was from a federal source in a nation where state and local agencies have the responsibility for education. While the focus of this series is certainly important to the United States (and other nations), it is not seen as important to schools.

These three projects also used an instructional design process through which the programs and related print materials could be developed, evaluated, and revised. In some cases the political process imposed itself, but with the best intention—that of getting the series used.

All three had the highest of production values, and the expectations for the projects were supported with large budgets. As a result, all were seen as highly appealing to students and teachers and obtained, at a minimum, an initial use in large numbers of classrooms. The continued use, however, was based on the programs' perceived utility in assisting teachers to reach their stated instructional goals.

The fourth example, "Scene," differs somewhat from the other three, being a continuing miscellany of programs not necessarily related to any special syllabus or project, Replacing a current affairs series, "Spotlight," or some years' standing, "Scene" was easily integrated into the notion wide service of broadcasts to schools whose general policy is laid clown by an Educational Broadcasting Council representative of the whole educational spectrum. Within these policy lines, program proposals are examined and accepted, modified or rejected by committees of educationalists appointed by the Council. They are normally subject to no other political pressures.

School producers have access to all the resources of the BBC and, subject to a modest but not illiberal budget, can go where they please for scriptwriters, presenters, actors, and production facilities. There are periodical postal surveys of audience size, and reactions to the programs are communicated by panel of reporting teachers and by visiting BBC liaison officers, extracts from whose reports have been given above.

Teachers receive printed notes indicating the aim and content of each program and the proposed treatment of the topic, together with some follow-up suggestions. Broadcasts may be fitted into an existing scheme of work but are often used as a starting point for discussion and to prompt initiatives like those described in the forgoing account of "James is our Brother."

In 1981, the "Scene" broadcasts were seen off air or on video-tape, regularly or selectively in 48 percent of British secondary schools. A number of the broadcasts have been repeated in the BBC's evening schedules for the general audiences by virtue of their human interest and the excellence of their production.

It is clear from previous experience 'that classroom television is not simply another audiovisual teaching device. It is too powerful and pervasive for that. The technology that supports it can, if desired, be used to support distance learning systems, adult education programs, the promotion of national identity, and the fostering of national culture. It can also be used, and in some countries has been used, for political purposes that do not always benefit education. Undoubtedly, classroom television serves education best when planners, curriculum specialists, teachers, and television', programmers work together to capitalize on the strengths of the medium and to diminish its weaknesses.

Classroom television is often thought of in the context of conventional broadcasting," but surely, within this century, it will benefit from such new technologies as cable television, direct broadcast satellite, videodiscs, and videocassette recorders. These will compensate for the inflexibility of broadcast program scheduling, which educators have sometimes found inconvenient.

Television is an expensive medium; in few instances has it reduced the cost of instruction. As Wilbur Schramm has noted in Big Media, Little Media: Tools and Technologies:

> One conclusion that emerges strongly is that systems, built around the broadcast media in particular, can be used with favourable economic results to extend and expand learning opportunities. In this case the media cost is not merely an add on to

> the normal cost of instruction, as supplementary media instruction might be, but can be compared directly with the cost of doing the same thing by conventional means.... If we can assume then, that favourable cost ratios can be expected from using media to do something that would otherwise have to be done by conventional means, what can we expect of the costs of simply adding media to ongoing class instruction? This is clearly an add on cost, to be justified, if at all, by its contribution to quality of instruction, unless it makes possible a reduction of some kind in present costs.

Many would argue that several television programs in this supplementary category do indeed contribute a significant additional quality, but the extra cost is difficult to justify unless it h, distributed over a large number of classrooms.

As educators and broadcasters feel increasing economic pressures, they are increasingly likely to look for less expensive methods of obtaining classroom television programs. One method is co-production, either among the states or provinces of one or two countries or among several countries. This can reduce the cost of the programs to each co-producer, and at the same time generate large enough audiences to justify the investment. Another method is the structured instructional use of entertainment programs—to increase students' motivation to read, to improve their comprehension of a foreign language, to complement social studies activities, and so on. Such use must involve assignments and interventions, either by teachers or teacher surrogates. Both the viewing of the program and some follow-up activity must be required and the focus must remain on education rather than entertainment.

Finally, some promising directions for future research must be mentioned. The effectiveness of television as a teaching device is no longer in doubt, Indeed, it has been verified so thoroughly that comparisons between the television classroom and the so-called traditional classroom are no longer interesting. Yet much remains to be learned about some elements of the learning situation.

While little research has been done in diversifying formats and production techniques, those of the Children's Television Workshop and other groups in the United States, Canada, Western Europe, and Japan have shown how differences in those elements, differently combined, variously affect students' learning and attitudes. In addition, developmental studies have shown how comprehension and learning vary with age. As children pass from one stage of cognitive development to another, their ability to perceive and use the content and organization of television programs grows more sophisticated.

Instructional design is now more important than ever in the production of classroom television. This greater importance has led to an increase in formative research, designed to improve the programs as they are being developed. More time and money are being spent to determine the needs and abilities of audiences before production and to test-run scripts, parts of programs, and whole programs in classrooms throughout production, Thus it is possible to revise one or a few programs in a series, if necessary, rather than the entire number.

10
Economics of Educational Technology

The production of educational services is a sector where the relationship between inputs and outcomes is much less clearly identifiable than in most other sectors of production of goods or services. What is the effect on educational results of a better qualified teacher, a lower pupil-teacher ratio, or educational media such as audiovisual aids, television programs, or computers? There is some evidence on these questions, but it is very often contradictory or inconclusive. These uncertainties are due to the variety of educational outcomes, and to the difficulty of measurement of most of them, in spite of some significant progress, at least in the measurement of cognitive achievements.

Most educational systems or educational institutions do not consider as a major and central objective the optimal use of inputs to maximize their outcomes, not only in public educational systems, but even in supposedly competitive private institutions. The survey carried out by Bowen among American colleges and universities leads to the conclusion that in higher education institutions, both private and public, unit costs are determined quite simply by the amount of money that can be raised from diverse sources: it is the "revenue theory of cost. The analysis of the relationship between expenditures (or costs) and outcomes (quantitative and qualitative) is basically inconclusive. It seems that the variance of costs is much higher than the variance of outcomes, which would mean that a certain number of institutions could have the same results with less resources. But on the other hand, the author argues that in its present trend, American higher education tends to be underfinanced and that the quality is declining.

These apparently contradictory results mean two things: there is it likely relation between available resources and academic excellency, but the right inputs remain to he specified. The provision of better educational services, leading to better educational results, requires more resources and is therefore more expensive. But more expensive educational services are not necessarily better ones if the right inputs have not been clearly identified.

Traditional teaching takes place in classrooms with a teacher facing students. The teacher has the main role, and the basic additional input is the use of textbooks. The concept of new educational technologies is applied to systems where the traditional system is either enriched, or completely redesigned, in order to provide a substitute for the traditional system. Such a substitute is essentially covered by the concept of distance education.

An important aspect of both enrichment in traditional schools and distance education is that they were not originally introduced to improve the cost-effectiveness ratio of educational systems. Enrichment is aimed at improving school performances, fighting against failures, dropouts, repetition rates, and so on. Distance education objective are mainly to provide access to education to excluded segments of the population: sick or handicapped people, mothers raising children, working people, adults who did not have the opportunity of studying while they were children, people living in remote areas, etc. The introduction of distance education for such target audiences was motivated principally by equity rather than economic considerations. The situation in the late 1980s is entirely different. Most countries, especially the poorest, are facing dramatic budgetary difficulties which have stopped the expansion of public resources allocated to education. This shrinking of resources for education accelerated in the second half of the 1970s and raised serious problems in satisfying it growing demand for educational services, More generally, after a quarter century of rapid expansion of public resources allocated to education, public authorities and public opinion are increasingly concerned with the idea of a "good" use of these resources, which explains the growing popularity of the concept of a "cost-effectiveness ratio" applied to educational services. This concept may be used for traditional teaching as well as for the so-called new educational technologies. Up to 1970, studies and data on the costs of these new educational technologies were very scanty, and usually based on inadequate or noncomparable methodologies. Rapid progress his been made during the 1970s, both methodologically and empirically, especially through the pioneering work of D.T. Jamison. The results of these efforts to measure costs are such that one tends to have more evidence oil cost comparisons than on results and outcomes.

In the first section or this entry, a description of the field of educational technology is provided, along with some tentative taxonomies; fit the second and third sections, the economics of the two main uses of this technology, namely within and out of school, are examined; and finally, in the fourth section, some additional information is given on a medium-by-medium basis.

Taxonomies of educational technology

The two great objectives of new educational technologies

were the improvement of school performances and the expansion of access to education of excluded groups. For an economist, the emphasis is rather on the potential changes in the productivity of educational services, namely to provide more or better services for a given budget, or to provide similar services at a lower cost.

Fortunately, this first dichotomy between new educational technologies in particularly adequate to fit with economic analysis. The introduction of new media within schools does not significantly modify the labour input (teaching staff) that exists in traditional teaching, One cannot expect, as a consequence, dramatic changes in terms of cost reductions. The typical case is characterized by a slight increase in costs, and potential changes in results, which are more likely when the former level was low than when it was already high or satisfactory.

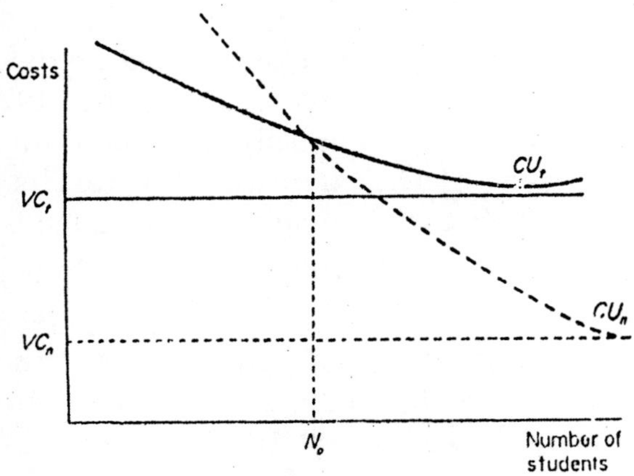

Figure 1: Unit costs in traditional teaching compared to distance education (CU_n)"

The second objective, however, opens large possibilities of changing the share of the labour input, The costs of a centralized production of didactic materials, printed or broadcasted, may be shared by a large number of' users, and as the fixed part of costs tends to be higher than in traditional systems, a large audience may substantially reduce the unit costs, where *FC* is the total fixed cost, *VC* the per student variable cost, and where the index *t* refers to traditional teaching and n to new educational technology. It appears clearly that above a certain number of students in the system (N_0), the unit costs in distance education are lower than in traditional teaching.

This cost behaviour suggests the taxonomy of new educational technologies. From an economic perspective, the differences between the two basic models are significant. The pupil-teacher ratio in distance education is much larger, and that means that the cost of labour is lower than in traditional teaching; as a result, it usually more than compensates the additional costs of supplementary teaching inputs. Finally, most of the study time is spent at home, and that reduces transportation and boarding costs.

Within-school applications of new educational technologies

Two main objectives have pushed the introduction of new educational inputs in the context of schools. The first is to improve school performances in a context of relatively qualified teachers, in order to help at least a certain number of students who tend to fail through lack of motivation, family support, or adequate cultural background. This model appears mostly in developed countries, where thousands of such projects have been implemented in the twentieth century, Tons of evaluation literature, poor and good, have been produced, but most are inconclusive on the effectiveness of such programs. The economic analysis of these projects has been dramatically neglected. In spite of the fact that the most costly programs, with motivated teachers, reinforced pedagogical teams, and access to a great variety of didactic supports, are likely to have measurable positive impact on school performances, there has not been a serious attempt either to relate these effects to costs, or to measure productivity changes. One of the pioneering countries in this field, Sweden, is experiencing a rapid decline in such use of educational technologies. This may be due, as Brusling argues, to new approaches in pedagogical ideologies, the use of technological devices being associated with an outdated Skinnerian and behaviourist theory, and to the development of more "participation-group-animation" types of pedagogical approach, in which hardware-type didactic inputs are used minimally. But another interpretation could be linked with the economic failure of these technologies, unable to demonstrate adequately any productivity increase. As a consequence, the tightening and shrinking of educational budgets in most countries, developed countries included, is rapidly killing these innovations.

The second objective is to improve school performances in a context of underqualified teachers, either inderqualified in general, or underqualified in specific fields. This case is more common in developing countries, where shortages in qualified teachers have been, and sometimes still are, particularly acute. From an economic point of view, the introduction of one or several audiovisual aids is supposed to compensate for the lack of teacher qualification, but in turn, such, teachers ought to be paid less than regularly qualified ones. Unfortunately, this last assumption has been rarely verified, except in it couple of Brazilian projects.

The two main media used in this context are television and radio. The focus was first placed on television on radio. As can be expected, radio is much cheaper' than television and the risk of a negative productivity effect is much lower. The majority of these projects have shown a positive impact on school performances and on access to education of previously excluded children. The question or cost effectiveness is less clear, except, that it is more likely to be positive with radio than with television.

Several of the above projects have already been closed. The Senegal pilot project will probably not be expanded, and the future of the Nicaraguan Radio Math is uncertain. In most cases, these closures are not due to a negative cost-effectiveness ratio, but to various sociopolitical factors, Even when financial difficulties have been emphasized, as in file case of Ivory Coast, they were actually minor compared with sociopolitical issues,

Some of the cost studies carried out on these systems and provides some evidence, mostly on within-school projects, where the basic auxiliary medium is television. The cost-effectiveness performances of these projects is not clearly demonstrated. Except in Mexico, where the costs are lower for similar results, the four other cases do not bring decisive improvements: a slight gain in school performances is obtained at the expense of a slight increase in unit costs. The results are somewhat better in Latin America than in Africa for two reasons: (a) supplementary costs of television are lower than in Africa because this technology is entirely mastered by local resources, while in Africa costly expatriate specialists have to be hired; (b) the labour qualification substitution is better obtained in Latin America, while in Africa such a substitution has not taken place.

Subsequent similar projects, based on radio instead of television, have been tried in Nicaragua, in the Philippines, and in Thailand. Radio is much cheaper than television, and above a rapidly reached audience threshold, unit costs tend to be negligible. As a consequence, when significantly positive performances appear, as is clearly the case in these three projects, one can reasonably assume that one has a positive cost effectiveness ratio.

The main conclusions we can draw from these economic evaluations are the following:

(a) Within-school educational technology has not dramatically improved the cost-effectiveness ratio of educational services compared with traditional teaching

(b) Radio is more likely to be cost effective than television, especially when carefully designed curricula are implemented.

(c) The labour qualification/media substitution, which assumes that underqualified teachers supported by media will be paid less to compensate media costs, is in most contexts unrealistic. Sometimes the opposite occurs: in the Ivory Coast, PETV's teachers have been promoted to higher salaries.

(d) The high death rate of within-school media projects is often due to teachers' rejection. This rejection may be explained by the rigidity of broadcast systems, and also by the fact that after some years of implementation, the underqualified teachers have assimilated the content of broadcast programs, and feel able to teach by themselves, without this now useless and constraining tool. Such an evolution may be seen as an unexpected result of this system i.e., a successful inservice training of teaching staff.

(e) From an economic and organizational perspective, such a result implies that such projects should be conceived of as temporary institutions, using part-time external consultants instead of a full-time permanent staff.

Out-of-school applications of new educational technologies

This field is the most promising area of the economically successful introduction of technology in education. While within-school technology is tending to decline, there is a rapid expansion of out-of-school systems, both formal and nonformal. There is a large variety of such systems, from simple and long-established correspondence courses to sophisticated multimedia projects, such as the now-famous Open University (UK), and in between, numerous nonformal educational projects in the field of hygiene and health habits, agricultural information, family planning, literacy and numeracy campaigns, etc. Several classifications of these systems are possible, according to the type of media used, the audience, the mode of studying, and the level of education.

Type of media

From an economic point of view, the differences in costs between the simplest correspondence course and a sophisticated multimedia system are target than the differences in effectiveness. The marginal productivity of each additional medium is therefore decreasing. But many authors argue that even if the additional impact of the last medium is lower than its costs, it may have significant external effects. For instance, in most open universities, the broadcasting of television programs is frequently considered by students as less important than printed material, in spite of the fact that it is substantially more expensive. But the broadcasting of these television programs generates useful external effects: large audiences, respectability, advertising possibilities, international recognition and exports of didactic material and pedagogical expertise.

Mode of studying

In contexts where the majority of' the target audience owns a receiver for the broadcasted programs at home, the reception may take place oil an individual basis but when this is not the case, the project has to organize a group study system, and to provide the receivers and the space. Very often the broadcasting is done early in the morning or late in the afternoon, when regular classrooms fire available. But there are many alternative to classrooms, such as a church or under a tree. Group study generally requires the presence of it monitor or "animateur," and is therefore more expensive than home study. On the other hand, group study provides more assistance, both from the monitors and from the peers, and stimulates the motivation of students more efficiently. There is relatively little evidence on the respective cost effectiveness of both systems, and the choice is very often dictated by contextual constraints.

Level of education

Since it radically reduces the face-to-face component or traditional teaching, distance education is more likely to succeed with students able to show some autonomy ill the learning process. As a consequence, young children are less able to follow these types of course than older children and adults. In practice it is difficult to enroll in such systems children below the age of 15. From an economic perspective, this is approximately the age from which forgone earnings call be estimated its private costs. Furthermore, for young children, the formal school system plays an additional role, which one could call a "child care" role, provided at no cost by the formal system as a by-product. This service would no longer be free under a home-study distance education system, and the economic advantage of a larger pupil-teacher ratio in distance education would be lost for children who still need the permanent presence of an adult, teacher or nonteacher.

Nevertheless, in developed countries the rapid

development of' microcomputers and the fact that many households possess these microcomputers as well as video recorders will increase the possibilities of individual instruction, young children included. However, the most appropriate level or education for distance education is clearly the university level, at which students have a solid basic background and can study by themselves. The second clear field or distance education is in nonformal education aimed at adults. Secondary education, especially at the senior level, and literacy programs for illiterate adults may be provided through distances education, but more easily with a system of group study than with it system of home study, in order to provide some minimal supervision and assistance.

Audience

The audience of distance education systems may theoretically be composed of the same age groups as formal systems for equivalent programs, as they were originally considered as equivalency programs, aimed at pupils who have missed the formal system for reasons such as sickness, social background, excessive private costs, distance, motherhood, etc. Distance education is a substitution system, some sort of second best to give a second chance to people excluded for nonacademic reasons. It is still exceptional to have a distance education system consideredas a normal, regular, find fully competitive alternative to traditional schools or universities, Primary-school teachers are another common audience for distance education projects, especially in developing countries where they are often underqualified. Such systems allow the retraining of these teachers without formal meetings in a single place, thus avoiding potentially high transportation costs.

It does not include several other available case studies, such as the Open University, the *French Tele-*

Enseignement or the Brazilian Logos II for inservice teacher training in these three cases, as in 8 out of 10 cases, costs per student and per graduate are lower than in equivalent format systems, with similar results. The proportion of fixed costs within the total cost is important, often exceeding 50 percent and reaching 90 percent n the case of Everyman University in Israel. The importance of fixed costs in the projects reviewed here should be seen in conjunction with what is to observed in traditional education where, for the most part, fixed costs, and administration costs are the same thing, the latter, however, being less "fixed" on the whole than production costs in media-based projects. The administration component is only slightly sensitive to marginal changes in system size (the same administrative unit being able to cope with an increase of up to, for example, 20 percent in system size' without having to increase its staff, and probably not needing to reduce its staff if system size is marginally reduced by, for example, up to 20 percent). On the other hand, a significant change in size necessarily involves ' a strengthening of the administration, Not only are the fixed costs of traditional education systems fixed 0 within a certain range, but they are also proportionally very low, administration costs rarely exceeding 10 percent of the total, This statement must however be corrected for certain institutional contexts. When teacher legislation does not allow the employing authority to relocate or dismiss teachers when reductions in staff are called for, labour costs tend to become almost a fixed item, which is possible only when it is the taxpayer who bears the bulk of education system costs.

Going back to the case of media systems, fixed production costs are real fixed costs. If a film costing $100,000 is seen by 1,000 pupils, the fixed production cost per pupil is $100; it if is seen :by 10,000, the cost falls to

$10 per head; if it is shown to 100,000 the cost is as low as $1; and if the number of viewers rises to 1,000,000 the cost per head falls to A negligible 10 cents.

This cost structure means that enrolment levels are of particular importance. For an equivalency program to succeed it must be assured of an appropriate minimum number of* students over a long enough period. To take one clear example, the Kenyan project has probably reached a stage where it no longer has enough students to justify its continuation; the Bahia project probably never will, if we take into account, the alternatives in Brazil, such as Minerva or *Telecurso*. It is, of course, impossible to set a precise figure for the minimum number of students as this varies from project to project. But at the level of secondary education, projects with fewer than 10,000 students per year are generally at risk, an; this figure may be a good enough estimate for general postsecondary education. Specialized vocationally oriented projects whose audience is dispersed and working may sometimes be justified with far fewer students, In this type of project, seen quite often in teacher retraining, the closest conventional alternative would show particularly high mii(costs, due mainly to:

(a) the need to assemble the participants in it single place, necessarily at a distance from where some of them reside;

(b) the need for participants to abandon their usual employment temporarily. and therefore to receive payment equal to their normal salaries,

(c) the additional cost of accommodation for nonresidents;

(d) possible cost of family accommodation, if the training course is a prolonged one, or the alternative psychological cost produced by the separation.

Under these circumstances the cost of the closest alternative is likely to be very high. In Kenya, for example, it was shown that the system could be economically justified if there were 2,000 enrollments for certificates.

In any event, the general figure of 10,000 should not be regarded as a rnagic threshold. The threshold will actually depend on four factors:

(a) the level of study;

(b) the choice between radio and television;

(c) the cost of die closest alternative;

(d) the degree to which the capital-labour substitution is extended.

These factors are linked. It is in adult education that the costs of the closest alternative me likely to be highest and where it is easiest to go much further ahead wall capital -labour substitution, since adults the more capable than young children of studying alone with the media, unassisted by a teacher. In this type of situation, a relatively modest number of students, say in the vicinity of 2,000, will justify a well-defined radio or radio-correspondence project economically. On the other hand at the primary and secondary levels, where the teacher is crucial, many more pupils are necessary before a positive cost-effectiveness ratio can be obtained, especially when television is the medium used. For these reasons it is important to look closely at the pupil target groups in a media project. Since many projects are experimental, or quasicxperimental, they involve small numbers of pupils, by definition, so that unit costs prove relatively high, since fixed costs must be spread over a small number of users. Projects that use television have highest unit costs. But television makes only a small difference to total costs where, despite the use of media, projects still rely to a great extent on teachers. An additional factor is that television costs vary greatly depending on whether the system utilizes an existing network at its marginal cost during off-peak times, or whet her it operates its own transmitter and its own network of ground relay transmitters. For out-of-school distance teaching projects it is impossible to use television unless numbers of the intended audience already own receivers.

Most of the projects studied her, are less expensive than equivalent traditional methods of education, especially if we take into account the fact that many of them are aimed at adults in employment who, by studying part time at a:, distance, avoid a loss or earnings while they study. This cost in salary would either be borne by the individual, who agrees to undergo training or retraining on a nonsalary basis (rate), or, its is more often the case by the employer, who continues to pay the trainee's salary but must find a replacement and therefore disburse two salaries on a single occupied work slot. For many such students these equivalency program systems are the only available way of studying. There was, however, substantial variation among projects in the extent to which they were cost saving, as compared with traditional education. Since the costs of both electronic and printed media are declining relative to the cost of teacher time, cost advantages for distance teaching can be expected to increase in the future.

Equivalency program projects seem to have a clear and positive impact on educational equity, in terms of making quality' education more widely available and of making access to any education at all possible for previously excluded groups.

The majority of projects in developing countries are relatively unsophisticated if one compares them to certain multimedia systems used in the developed countries. This simplicity has proved a sound choice. It is clear that a systematic quest for programs of high artistic quality would have swung the cost-effectiveness ratio to [lie negative side, something particularly true of television-based systems. All the school television projects described here, except Telecurso, are the work of absolutely minimal production teams, perhaps 10 times smaller than similar professional groups in the high-income countries, The achievement of professional standards while maintaining a good cost-effectiveness ratio would he possible only if enrollments were far more numerous. In most cases, television personnel have gained their experience on the job, so that it certain amateurism is it feature of the production studios. If, instead of making do with modest local talent, reliance had been placed on it large complement of technicians from high-income countries, it is likely that, In the absence of a significant increase in enrollments, the cost-effectiveness ratio would again been an inverse one.

Further comments on the economics of some specific media

Several means have been introduced in conventional schools to improve the quality of teaching services. A common belief among educators is that the reduction of the number of pupils per teacher is the most appropriate solution to improve the quality of their teaching. From an empirical point of view, this point remains today highly controversial. Most studies do not show significant changes in student performances associated with class size. Some others tend to show that some slight improvements can be reached when the average number of students goes from 40 to 20, and more substantial improvements below, especially around 10, but this solution is clearly impractical in most developing countries because of its cost implications.

One word should be said concerning the provision of textbooks, It is not a new medium, but its cost-effectiveness ratio remains remarkable. In it school context where a substantial proportion of pupils have no access to textbooks, the free provision of textbooks has a relatively small effect on the per student cost and a significant impact on cognitive performances. A review is given below of the potential impact of the never media used in classes, that is, radio, television, language, laboratories, and computers.

Radio

Radio is by far the cheapest means to reach a wide audience. A study on Malawi has shown that to provide relevant information and training to farmers, an hour of contact by radio is 3,000 times cheaper than face-to-face communication. When radio sets are widespread, the use of radio for informal educational programs is certainly appropriate. But it can also be used for in-class " direct teaching in some fields, such as mathematics, when primary teachers are unsufficiently qualified, or for the retraining of teachers themselves, Finally, radio can be used for distance teaching systems, especially for equivalency programs. This last point will be expanded below.

Language laboratories

The introduction of language laboratories in school institutions in most developed countries has produced rather disappointing results. Their pedagogical impact is usually not statistically significant and the per student-costs tend to be high. The hourly student cost is, for instance in the case of France, around US$4, of which half is due to the language laboratory itself, and half due to additional teaching staff, because the class has to be divided into two groups. Furthermore, the utilization of these language laboratories follows the traditional school rhythm, instead of intensive periods of learning during a short period of time. This means usually 1 hour every 2 weeks, which tends to be too long an interval between two sessions to produce significant results, Very likely, the utilization of language laboratories will tend to encourage free access by students and a more intensive rate of utilization. It is also possible that language-teaching computers will be developed for autonomous learning.

Television

Great expectations were placed oil the introduction of television programs in education. A wide range of experience has been gained around the world with uneven success. Today, the feelings of decision makers in educational systems concerning the advantages of using television in formal education are rather mixed. It is therefore necessary to try to clarify what we have learned from these experiences and what we can predict for the future.

(a) *The question of the costs and quality of television programs.* 12 educational projects using television programs, the yearly number of program hours produced and the average cost of production of a one-hour program. Of course, some of these figures arc out of date, but the most surprising overall result is the very large variability of the cost of a unit of output.

The nature of the programs produced in these different projects may vary considerably, In the case of Stanford University, it is a live production of a professor giving a lecture; while in the case of, the Open University, one has sophisticated programs with professional standards similar to the British Broadcasting Corporation (BBC) programs, In between, there are a variety of television productions, managed either by nonprofessional television people, mainly retrained teachers, or by semi-professional or professional television specialists. Using professional television criteria, it is possible to find a close relation between the unit costs of these different television programs and their technical quality. But the relation between the cost and/ or t; quality of educational television programs and their pedagogical impact is much less close. In any case, even if it were possible to show that technically good programmes have a better pedagogical impact, there is no chance that the differences of impact may have the same range as of costs. This means that with a given budget constraint, it is rational to sacrifice some technical quality in favour of other educational material.

(b) *Computer-assisted instruction.* The recent development of microcomputing systems has raised great expectations. Nevertheless, their introduction in the educational systems has to be carefully evaluated. In spite of a rapid decline of the costs of the hardware, the costs per student remain relative high: most projects show hourly per student costs around US$4, and as long as the software costs cannot be shared by a great number of students, it is unlikely to have a positive cost-effectiveness ratio in the context of most developing countries in the near future, except for some specific reasons, namely; (a) the teaching of computer science should rapidly be undertaken, to avoid the building of a new gap between developed and developing countries in a strategic field; and (b) the teaching of foreign languages may very soon become cost effective with computers. That does not mean that developing countries themselves should invest in the development of this material, but they should be ready to use, at a relatively low marginal cost, what is implemented in this field in richer countries.